THIS BOOK
BELONGS TO

_____

# A LITTLE GOD TIME

## FOR Kids

## BroadStreet KIDS

BroadStreet Kids
Savage, Minnesota, USA
BroadStreet Kids is an imprint of BroadStreet Publishing Group, LLC.
Broadstreetpublishing.com

# A Little God Time for Kids

© 2019 by BroadStreet Publishing®

ISBN 978-1-4245-5839-1 (faux)
ISBN 978-1-4245-5517-8 (e-book)

Devotional entries composed by Janelle Breckell.

Design by Chris Garborg | garborgdesign.com
Edited and compiled by Michelle Winger | literallyprecise.com

Printed in China.

17  18  19  20  21  22  23      7  6  5  4  3  2  1

The LORD is merciful
and compassionate,
slow to get angry and
filled with unfailing love.
The LORD is good
to everyone.
He showers compassion
on all his creation.

PSALM 145:8-9 NLT

# Introduction

God created you for a reason.
There is no one quite like you,
and he is delighted to call
you his very own. Let joy and
peace come into your heart
as you spend a little time with
God each day.

# JANUARY

Blessed are those you choose
and bring near to worship you.
You bring us into the courtyards
of your holy temple.
There in your house we are filled
with all kinds of good things.

PSALM 65:4 NIRV

# Shiny and New

*Anyone who belongs to Christ has become a new person. The old life is gone; a new life has begun!*
2 CORINTHIANS 5:17 NLT

Have you ever seen a very dirty car go through a car wash and come out sparkling clean? When we accept Jesus into our hearts, he forgets all the bad, ugly things we have done, and he makes us shiny and new—like that nice clean car.

We all have bad things we would like to forget, like mean words we've said and people we've hurt. Every day, we can tell Jesus we are sorry for our sin and he washes that yucky dirt away.

*God, I'm so happy that you can take my sin away. Thank you for forgiving me and making me clean.*

# Just Pray

*Then that person can pray to God*
*and be blessed by him.*
*They will see God's face and shout for joy.*
*God will make them well and happy again.*

JOB 33:26 NIRV

What do we have to do to be accepted by God? Do we need to be perfect? No, we just need to pray. When we pray to God, it's like he puts his arms around us and gives us a big hug.

It doesn't matter how you feel about yourself, God loves you very much. He sees you, he hears you, and he loves spending time with you.

*God, thank you for loving me and accepting me just the way I am.*

# Beautiful Things

*The earth and everything in it belong to the Lord.*
*. The world and all its people belong to him.*
PSALM 24:1 ICB

Picture this. The sky is gray. Rain is falling, and you trip in a mud puddle. You had friends at your house last night and your mom is mad that they left your room messy. You can't see anything beautiful around you.

Now close your eyes. Say this name: Jesus. Now open them, and look again. Do you see that little spot of blue sky, that single ray of light sneaking through the clouds? Do you notice the beautiful water drops resting on the bushes? Remember all the fun you had with the friends who made the mess? We can always find something beautiful if we look for it.

*Jesus, when I say your name, I see beautiful things all around me. Thank you for making such awesome things.*

# Good Gifts

*Whatever is good and perfect is a gift coming down to us from God our Father, who created all the lights in the heavens. He never changes.*

JAMES 1:17 NLT

Count your blessings. That might be something you hear a lot, but do you know what it means? Every good thing in our lives is a blessing from God. Think of every good thing you possibly can.

Maybe today is hard. Maybe you feel like there are more bad things than good. It's okay. Just start counting your blessings anyway. You might be surprised by how many there are!

**Heavenly Father, you give everyone wonderful gifts. Thank you that you never change. You send down blessings like rays of light.**

# Ask Anything

*Here is what we can be sure of when we come to God in prayer. If we ask anything in keeping with what he wants, he hears us. If we know that God hears what we ask for, we know that we have it.*

1 JOHN 5:14-15 NIRV

Can you think of a time when you really wanted something but you were afraid to ask? Why were you afraid? Did you think you hadn't been good enough to get it? It can be hard to ask for what you want.

When you make God the most important person in your life, you can ask him for anything. You don't need to be afraid. He likes it when you ask him things. He loves to hear your voice.

**God, I want you more than anything in the world. I feel so safe when I ask you for things. You always give me what I need.**

# Cry Like a Baby

*As a mother comforts her child,*
*I will comfort you.*
ISAIAH 66:13-14 NIRV

It's okay to cry like a baby sometimes. There are days when lots of things don't go your way: someone is unkind to you, or you fall off your bicycle, or you feel afraid.

It's okay to close your eyes and snuggle deep into God's arms. He wants you there! Listen to him tell you how much he loves you. Let him gently rock you, and fill you with peace.

*God, I need you to hold me and love me and tell me everything's going to be okay today. Thank you for loving me even when I cry like a baby.*

# A Safe Place

*My God is my rock.*
*I can run to him for safety.*
*The LORD saves me from those*
*who want to harm me.*
2 SAMUEL 22:3 NCV

Sometimes we feel like we are in the middle of a battle. Just as we find shelter from the arrows, spears start to fly at us. When the Old Testament was written, these battles were real wars: the arrows and spears were real.

Today, the arrows might be more like bullies, hard homework, or fighting parents. But your hiding spot should always be the same. God is your safe place. Whenever you run to him, he is ready to protect you.

**God, you are my protector. Thank you for your promise to rescue me. I can find peace in your love.**

# Lots of Questions

*You will teach me God's way to live.*
*Being with you will fill me with joy.*
*At your right hand I will find pleasure forever.*
PSALM 16:11 ICB

There are some days when we have a lot of questions. There are many things that we don't understand. Asking parents for help is pretty easy. They usually have good answers.

Did you know that God gave you someone who can answer all of your questions? The Holy Spirit is here to help us. He shows us what to do, and he fills us with joy.

*Holy Spirit, thank you that you can answer all my questions. I trust you to show me what I need to know. I want to be filled with your joy.*

# Lifetime Guarantee

*I truly believe
I will live to see the LORD's goodness.
Wait for the LORD's help.
Be strong and brave
and wait for the LORD's help.*
PSALM 27:13-14 ICB

What do you do when you get really sick? Usually you go to the doctor because you trust that they will help you to get better. We know that good doctors will give us the advice or medicine that we need to help, but sometimes it takes a while to work!

God is like a good doctor that we can trust to help us. We go to him and ask him to help make us strong because we believe that he cares so much for us.

**God, thank you that I can trust you to help me any time that I come to you and ask. Help me to have courage because I know that you care for me.**

# Twirling with Joy

*You changed my sorrow into dancing.
You took away my clothes of sadness,
and clothed me in happiness.
I will sing to you and not be silent.
LORD, my God, I will praise you forever.*

PSALM 30:11-12 NCV

Was there ever a time when you lost something and were really sad, and then you found it and became really happy? The Bible says that God can help us to turn our sadness into happiness!

Sometimes we like to sing or shout when we are happy, sometimes we like to dance. When God turns your sadness into happiness, you won't be able to be quiet, you will want to praise him!

**Lord, thank you that you can fill my heart with joy. I will sing, dance, and praise you because you are good to me.**

# Truly Awesome

*The heavens were made*
*when the LORD commanded it to happen.*
*All the stars were created by the breath of his mouth.*
*He gathers together the waters of the sea.*
*He puts the oceans in their places.*

PSALM 33:6-7 NIRV

Have you ever tried to make something happen just by wishing it, or maybe even whispering it? Maybe you have said, "Sun, please come out," or, "Ball, get into the goal!" Well, God did this when he made the universe—he just spoke the words, and it happened!

God is powerful and awesome! He can hold an ocean in his hand, and also know every hair on your little head. He is a God who can do big things, and a God that loves little things… especially you!

*Lord God, when I think about how your words created the universe, and how the huge oceans are like little jars in your storehouse, I am so amazed! You are awesome!*

17

# Only for You

*No king is saved by his great army.*
*No warrior escapes by his great strength.*
*Horses can't bring victory.*
*They can't save by their strength.*
*But the Lord looks after those who fear him.*
*He watches over those who put their hope in his love.*

PSALM 33:16-18 ICB

Not everyone who can sing well will become famous. The fastest runner at your school might not make it to the Olympics. Sometimes we think that to be the best means that the whole world will notice us. But God didn't give us gifts so that we could be famous; he gave us gifts so that we can show the world his love.

What things are you really good at? God wants you to do your best with the skills that he has given you, but most of all, he wants you to do it with a good heart.

**God, I thank you for the gifts you have given me, and I will do my best, trusting you will show me how to use them for your good.**

# Be Healed

*With you is the fountain of life;*
*in your light we see light.*
Psalm 36:9 NRSV

When you're thirsty, do you run to the desert or the fountain? If you are stumbling around in the dark, do you look for the light switch, or squeeze your eyes shut? When we need help, we are pretty good at knowing where to go!

God is like a lamp, lighting up the way we should go. He is like a water fountain, giving us new strength when we need it. All we have to do is come to him, because he can't help us if we don't let him.

*Heavenly Father, sometimes I forget to ask you for help when I need it the most. Remind me to come to you when I need strength, because I trust that you will help me.*

# All Comfort

*God is our merciful Father and the source of all comfort. He comforts us in all our troubles so that we can comfort others. When they are troubled, we will be able to give them the same comfort God has given us.*
2 CORINTHIANS 1:3-5 NLT

There are many ways that we can make ourselves feel better when we are sad. Sometimes food, a bath, a game, or fun music can help. God has given us a lot of good things in life, but the very best comfort we get is when we talk to him.

Did you know that God understands all of your troubles? Remember that he created you and sees you, every single day. The next time you are feeling sad, tell God about it. He will make a way for you to feel stronger and happier.

*Heavenly Father, thank you that I can always talk to you when I feel upset. Thank you that you care so much about me and that you are always with me.*

# Beyond Sight

*Wherever I am, though far away at the ends of the earth, I will cry to you for help. When my heart is faint and overwhelmed, lead me to the mighty, towering Rock of safety.*

PSALM 61:2 TLB

Have you ever tried to get through a paper maze? You might have even been in a real maze. Sometimes you get stuck. You hit a dead end, or go around in circles. Life can feel a little bit like that—you can feel lost or stuck.

The amazing thing about God is that he always knows where you are! You just need to call out to him and ask for help. He can tell you the way by letting you know the right direction.

*Lord, how cool it is to know that when I am lost, I can call out to you. Your voice will be my help and your hands will pick me up.*

# So Thirsty

*O God, you are my God; I seek you,*
*my soul thirsts for you;*
*my flesh faints for you,*
*as in a dry and weary land*
*where there is no water.*

PSALM 63:1 NRSV

Have you ever been playing for so long that all the sudden you feel like you would fall over if you didn't have any water? When you are that thirsty, all you can think about is getting a drink!

This Bible verse compares wanting God to being that thirsty. We might not feel like that right now, but the more we get to know God, the more we realize we need him—just like that drink of water!

*Lord, help me to understand how*
*much I need you. I want to have*
*more of your help, your goodness,*
*and your strength in my life.*

# Better than Life

*Your unfailing love is better than life itself;
how I praise you!*
PSALM 63:3 NLT

What are your favorite things in life? Is it your bike, or perhaps it's ice-cream, a roller-coaster, playing sports, or just being with friends. It might be all of those things! Did you know that God created those? He wanted us to enjoy life because he loves us. That's kind of what this verse is saying—that his love is better than life, because his love created all the great things in life.

The next time you are really enjoying something that you love, remember that God created it for you. And then remember to thank him for it.

*Lord, nothing compares to your love. Help me to thank you for all the things in life that I enjoy, because I know they come from you.*

# Make My Day

*Fill us with your love every morning.*
*Then we will sing and rejoice all our lives.*
PSALM 90:14 NCV

Why is it important to have breakfast in the morning? Your parents will probably tell you that you need to eat a good breakfast because it will give you energy for the rest of the day.

It's a good thing to start your day with Jesus too. Just reading a little bit from the Bible, or praying that he will help you today, is a really good start to your day. It will give you the strength that you need to get through your day!

*Jesus, I invite you to make my day. When I am frustrated or unhappy, give me patience and joy. Fill me with your love so I can love other people around me.*

# His Sheep

*Know that the Lord is God.*
*He made us, and we belong to him.*
*We are his people, the sheep he tends*
PSALM 100:3 ICB

Do you own a pet, or know some friends who do? Pets are neat! You can play with them, give them commands, and sit next to them when you are lonely. In Bible times, people had sheep to take care of—not like big farms that we see today—often just a few sheep at a time. They must have come to love their sheep like pets.

This Bible verse says that we are like God's sheep. He cares about us the same way that you might care for a pet. He wants to be with us and take care of us every day.

*Father God, I know that you really care about me, and that you want to enjoy me, and be with me. Help me to remember that I am yours.*

# Laid Low

*Give me life, as you have promised.*
PSALM 119:25 ICB

Even people in the Bible felt upset sometimes. It's okay to feel upset, and it's okay to say that you are upset. Maybe a friend has been mean to you, or your parents yelled at you, or you were left out of a game. Maybe you didn't play well at your sports game this week.

Don't give up! God knows when you are upset and he cares when you feel bad. When you are discouraged, it's time to ask God to speak to you. Do you know what he will say? He will say that he loves you, and that he is there for you.

***Dear Lord, in those times when I am most upset, help me to ask you for your words of truth. Thank you that you will encourage me with your love.***

# Your Ways

*Keep me from looking at worthless things.*
*Let me live by your word.*
PSALM 119:37 NCV

Have you ever bought a really cheap toy, only to have it break a few hours later? Sometimes things can look good in the store but they are not high quality. When you eat a lot of junk food that looks good, you soon realize that you don't feel very good.

There are actually a lot of things in life that aren't worth having. That's why it's important to find out what God says is important, because he is the one that loves you and knows what is best for you.

***Jesus, help me to figure out what things in life are worthless, and what things are truly good for me. Help me to find these things in the Bible.***

# In a Season of Suffering

*When I suffer, this comforts me:*
*Your promise gives me life.*
PSALM 119:50 ICB

Sometimes life is not fair. Like when someone blames you when it wasn't your fault. Or someone has made fun of you for the way you look. You might have embarrassed yourself playing sports. Perhaps your parents are fighting and it makes you afraid. There are a lot of things that can upset you.

Guess what? Jesus has made a promise to always be with you. He sent the Holy Spirit, our helper, to whisper to us when things go wrong and remind us that we are loved by him.

*Lord, when I feel really upset, let me hear the Holy Spirit reminding me of your promises. Thank you that you watch over my life.*

# The Gift in the Struggle

*My suffering was good for me,*
*for it taught me to pay attention to your decrees.*
PSALM 119:71 NLT

It's no fun being sent to your room for doing something wrong. It doesn't feel great spending time by yourself. After a while, you calm down and maybe you even forget why you were angry.

It's important to learn that discipline is good for us. It's good for us to take some time out and think about our feelings. God can always speak to us when we are quiet and listening.

*Lord God, help me to understand that*
*sometimes it is better to be disciplined than*
*to keep on doing the wrong thing. Help me*
*to pay attention to you!*

# The Path to Peace

*Those who love your teachings will find true peace.*
*Nothing will defeat them.*
PSALM 119:165 ICB

Have you ever wanted to cheat on a game so you could win? Or cross the road in the wrong place just to get to the other side quicker? Maybe you won't wear a helmet because you think it looks silly. Following rules is sometimes hard!

God made up some rules—not to make it hard for you, but to keep you safe, and keep others safe around you. When you love God's rules, it means that you trust that he knows what is best for you, and that gives you a lot of peace!

*Lord, I want to please you and keep your rules because I know that I will be a more peaceful person when I live by your goodness.*

# Get Wise

*Getting wisdom is the wisest thing you can do!*
*And whatever else you do, develop good judgment.*
PROVERBS 4:7 NLT

If you couldn't find a trash can, would you throw your garbage on the ground? If you didn't know the answer to a question at school, would you look at someone else's answer? If you saw someone drop their money, would you pick it up and keep it?

We have to make decisions so many times in one day! The Bible says that we need to get wisdom. When we ask for wisdom, we choose to do the right thing. And we usually know what that is because we know what Jesus would do.

**Father God, help me to make good decisions and to be wise in all that I do.**

# Rock Solid

*"The rain came down, the streams rose, and the winds blew and beat against that house; yet it did not fall, because it had its foundation on the rock."*

MATTHEW 7:25 NIV

Sometimes life is like a huge storm. It beats down, tosses you around, and carries you away in a flood of troubles and worries. It seems like bad stuff happens all at once. When bad things happen, who do you run to?

The Bible says that the best way to make sure you can stand tall in a storm is to know about God and to have faith in his promises. Then you will be like a house that has a strong foundation and will not break in a storm.

*Lord Jesus, I know that no matter what I face, I will not fall if you are with me. I choose to believe this today.*

# The Me You See

*Mary responded, "I am the Lord's servant.
May everything you have said about me come true."
And then the angel left her.*

LUKE 1:38 NLT

A lot of people say that Mary was quite young when the angel came to tell her that she would one day have baby, and that the baby would be Jesus. That must have been really scary!

Instead of running away, Mary believed God, and said that she would do what God wanted her to do. God used Mary as part of his plan to save the world—everything the angel said came true. Will you believe God's plan for your life?

*Father God, show me that you have important things for me to do in this world. I want to obey you and follow your ways.*

33

# So Much Love

*While they were throwing stones, Stephen prayed,
"Lord Jesus, receive my spirit!" He fell on his knees
and cried in a loud voice, "Lord, do not hold this sin
against them!" After Stephen said this, he died.*
ACTS 7:59-60 ICB

If someone were throwing stones at you, would
you just stand there and pray for them? Probably not!
But that's just what Stephen in the Bible did. He knew
that the people that were hurting him did not really
understand God. Stephen forgave them for hurting him.

Have you been hurt by people before? Take some
time today to forgive them. Tell Jesus that you want
these people to know his love.

*Lord, fill me with the peace that
Stephen had. Help me to so
wrapped in your love, that I can
forgive those who hurt me.*

# Even Better Things

*"No one has ever seen this.*
*No one has ever heard about it.*
*No one has ever imagined*
*what God has prepared for those*
*who love him."*
1 CORINTHIANS 2:9 ICB

Consider the most beautiful thing you've ever seen. Remember, or listen to, the most wonderful song you've ever heard. Imagine the most perfect day possible. It's amazing, right?

Guess what? God has even better things in store for you! No dream even comes close. And the best part is that Jesus is preparing all this goodness for you, right now. One day you will see and feel it all. You have a great future to look forward to.

*Lord, thank you for all the beauty around me.*
*Remind me that there are even more beautiful*
*things to come.*

# A Special Gift

*If the whole body were an eye, where would the hearing be? If the whole body were hearing, where would the sense of smell be? But as it is, God arranged the members in the body, each one of them, as he chose.*

1 CORINTHIANS 12:17-18 NCV

Have you ever heard a beautiful singer or seen an amazing artist and wanted to do what they do? Those feelings are normal. We all want to be talented. But if we keep wanting someone else's gifts, we'll forget about our own.

God has given everyone different gifts so that we can all work together. Imagine a band that had only drums. A great band has all different instruments. Imagine a soccer team that has only goal keepers. A great team has different positions and strengths. The world needs your special gift. Find it and use it!

**Father, show me what gifts you have blessed me with and help me to use them for your good.**

# When Things Get Hard

*I begged the Lord three times to take this problem away from me. But he said to me, "My grace is enough for you. When you are weak, my power is made perfect in you."*
2 CORINTHIANS 12:8-9 NCV

You make the team and then break a bone and have to spend all season on the bench. One of your parents is sick and God is not healing them. Your best friend moves away and now you have to find a new group of friends. What is going on? Does God want you to struggle?

God does not want anyone to be hurt, but he does use hard times to show us his power and make us better people. Maybe losing that friend means you found a great, new group of friends that you have for the rest of your life! God can turn hard things into good things.

**Lord God, help me to see that you can use my weakness to do something great. I will trust you and praise you in that.**

37

# FEBRUARY

Don't remember the sins I committed
when I was young.
Don't remember how often
I refused to obey you.
Remember me because you love me.
Lord, you are good.

PSALM 25:7 NIRV

# Still My Thoughts

*When you are angry, do not sin.*
*And do not go on being angry all day.*
*Do not give the devil a way to defeat you.*
EPHESIANS 4:26-27 ICB

When was the last time you felt so angry that you wanted to kick something or throw things around the room? It's pretty normal to feel angry about things, but you have to be careful about what you do with that anger.

What would happen if you hurt yourself, or someone else, or damaged something while you were angry? It would make the situation worse, right? That's why God's way says to find a way to calm down so that you don't keep thinking about your anger. Ask Jesus to help you settle down, and then do something else— like read a book, write a letter, or kick a ball around!

*Father God, help me to let go of my anger.*
*Give me ways to do something right*
*when I am angry instead*
*of something that I will*
*regret. Thank you for*
*your forgiveness.*

# Trading Worry for Peace

*Don't worry about anything; instead, pray about everything. Tell God what you need, and thank him for all he has done. Then you will experience God's peace, which exceeds anything we can understand.*
PHILIPPIANS 4:6-7 NLT

Have you ever played with trading cards? You give your friends the extras that you have, and they give you cards that you are missing. This is kind of like what God asks us to do with our worries. He can take your worry, and give you back peace!

What things do you worry about? Is it homework, making friends, or finding a lost toy? Tell Jesus about it, and ask him to help you feel peaceful because you know that he cares.

**Lord Jesus, I bring my worries to you and ask you to help me. Thank you for your promise of peace.**

# Small Things

*I know how to live when I am poor, and I know how to live when I have plenty. I have learned the secret of being happy at any time in everything that happens, when I have enough to eat and when I go hungry, when I have more than I need and when I do not have enough.*

PHILIPPIANS 4:12 NCV

We have favorite dinners, and meals that we don't like very much. Can you think of a favorite dinner of yours? Now think of someone who doesn't get dinners at all. That's pretty sad, right? It's good to be thankful for every meal that you get, even if you don't like it very much.

Paul, from the Bible, said that he was okay even when he was put in prison and didn't have very much. That's because he was thankful for every little thing that Jesus had given him. We can learn to be thankful, no matter how much or how little we have.

**Jesus, help me to be happy with whatever I have, even if it is only a little.**

# God Is Real

*You have not seen Christ, but still you love him.*
*You cannot see him now, but you believe in him.*
*You are filled with a joy that cannot be explained.*
*And that joy is full of glory.*

1 PETER 1:8 ICB

How do you know that the wind is real? You can't see it, but you can hear it, feel it, and see what it does to clouds and trees. God is kind of like the wind—we don't see him, but we feel and see what his love does to our lives and other people's lives.

It's pretty amazing to love someone that you can't see, but the Bible says that when you love God, you will be filled with a lot of joy. So smile, because you love God, and he loves you!

*God, I know that you are real.*
*Sometimes I can't explain it,*
*but I love you, because I know*
*that you love me. Thank you for*
*your joy that makes me smile.*

# Try Not to Fight

*Be sure that no one pays back wrong for wrong.*
*But always try to do what is good for each other*
*and for all people.*
1 Thessalonians 5:15 icb

When someone shoves you, do you shove back?
If they say something mean, are you mean too? No
matter who starts a fight, everyone who is involved
will probably get in trouble.

It's hard to not fight back, but that's just what God
wants us to do. He doesn't want the problem to get
worse, so he asks us to do good for each other, even
to people who are not very nice. And you will feel
better when you choose to do the right thing.

*Holy Spirit, fill me with your goodness.*
*Help me not to fight back but to forgive*
*and to try to be good to all people.*

# Pray for Others

*That is why we always pray for you. We ask our God to help you live the good way that he called you to live. The goodness you have makes you want to do good, and the faith you have makes you work. We pray that with his power God will help you do these things more and more.*

2 Thessalonians 1:11 icb

Have you ever had someone pray for you? Maybe it was kids at church or someone in your family. It feels good to be prayed for, doesn't it? God wants us to pray for each other because prayer shows people love.

Sometimes we are embarrassed to pray out loud. That's okay! You can always pray for people in your own quiet times, or in your head. Whatever way you pray, God will reward you with faith. You can be sure that God hears your prayers!

*Dear Jesus, remind me to pray for other people. Give me courage when I need to pray out loud and help me to know that you are always listening.*

# More than Gold

*These troubles come to prove that your faith is pure. This purity of faith is worth more than gold. Gold can be proved to be pure by fire, but gold can be destroyed. But the purity of your faith will bring you praise and glory and honor when Jesus Christ comes again.*

1 PETER 1:7 ICB

Did you know that gold is one of the most precious metals because it is one of the strongest and shiniest? Gold doesn't just come out of the ground like that though; it has to be cleaned with fire!

God says that our belief in Jesus is like gold. It is very precious and very strong. It's important that we see our faith as a treasure just like a piece of gold.

***God, please help me to know just how precious and strong my faith is.***

# He Cares About It!

*Give all your worries to him, because he cares for you.*
1 PETER 5:7 ICB

Imagine building a tower of stones. You put one stone on top of the other until the tower gets wobbly and comes crashing down. That's what can happen when we let all of our little worries build up. It's much better to deal with one worry at a time so that things don't feel like they are crashing down around us!

Jesus says that he cares so much for you. You can take every little worry to him. It doesn't matter if it's a big deal or not; Jesus cares about what worries you. So talk to him. You will feel better when you do.

*Jesus, I don't want to be worried about everything anymore. Help me to talk to you whenever I get anxious. I know that you care for me.*

# In His Light

*Life was in him, and that life was the light for all people. The light shines in the darkness. But the darkness has not overcome the light.*

JOHN 1:4-5 NIRV

What do you need when it's really, really dark? A light, of course! Sometimes things we are sad or worried about feel like darkness. The Bible says that Jesus is like a light in these times.

Nothing is more powerful than the light of God's Word. His love never fails and his promises last forever. Nothing can keep you from his love.

**Lord Jesus, you are light—beautiful and shining. When things feel dark, help me to find hope in your light.**

# Worth It

*"It was not that this man sinned, or his parents, but that the works of God might be displayed in him."*

JOHN 9:3 ESV

Back in the time of Jesus, when people were sick, others would say they were sick because they had done something wrong. Jesus' disciples thought this way about a blind man, but Jesus explained it differently. Right before he healed the man's eyes, Jesus said the man was blind so that people would see God's power.

Sometimes we can go through hard things, like the blind man did, so people can see that God is still good. When we get better, we can tell others that God helped us during our hard times.

*Lord, I know my troubles can turn out for the best. Help me to trust you and to tell people about your goodness.*

# Heart Directions

*We pray that the Lord will lead your hearts into God's love and Christ's patience.*

2 THESSALONIANS 3:5 ICB

Think of a time you may have run ahead of your parents at the fair or zoo, only to realize you had no idea where you were going. We can get lost if we don't listen to directions, and that can be scary!

Our heart needs direction too. Sometimes we don't know how to feel, or we don't know the right thing to do. This is when we can stop, and ask God to help. He will be able to give us the answers that we need and fill us with love.

**Lord, my heart needs directions.**
**Fill me with your love, and lead me to you.**

# Bring You Back

*"I will let you find me," says the Lord. "And I will bring you back from your captivity. I forced you to leave this place. But I will gather you from all the nations. I will gather you from the places I have sent you as captives," says the Lord. "And I will bring you back to this place."*

JEREMIAH 29:14 ICB

Have you ever dropped a handful of marbles and seen them roll in different directions? That's kind of like what happened to God's people in the Bible. After a while, God made a promise to those people: the Israelites. He said that he would gather them all back up toward him.

We can feel like those marbles at times, separated from God and from others. God's promise is for you too. He will find you and bring you back. You are never far from his sight, or his reach.

*Father, sometimes it feels like I've lost you, but I know that you haven't lost me! Please bring me close to you.*

# Free to Rest

*Those who respect the Lord will live
and be content, unbothered by trouble.*
PROVERBS 19:23 ICB

Sometimes fearing things means that we understand that they are powerful—like a lion, or huge waves crashing on the beach. But lions and waves are beautiful, aren't they? That's what God means when he says to fear him—it means you know that he is powerful.

That same, powerful God, is the one that watches over you and protects you. He is so big that you know that being on his side means you are safe!

**Lord, thank you that you are powerful.
I know that means that I am safe with you.**

# Speaking Truth

*It is better to correct someone openly
than to love him and not show it.
The slap of a friend can be trusted to help you.
But the kisses of an enemy are nothing but lies.*

PROVERBS 27:5-6 ICB

It is always better to tell the truth. It might be easier to lie sometimes, but it never feels good on the inside. Even though it is hard to tell the truth, you feel a lot better when you do. When you are always truthful, people can trust you.

The next time you want to tell a lie, remember that it will only make you feel worse. Speaking the truth is the best way. It keeps you and others from getting hurt. God loves truth, and he loves you!

**God, help me to be brave enough to always tell the truth. Thank you for forgiving me and loving me, no matter what.**

# keep Going

*Whether you turn to the right or to the left,*
*your ears will hear a voice behind you, saying,*
*"This is the way; walk in it."*
ISAIAH 30:21 NIV

Should I keep playing soccer? Is this friend good for me? Should I finish my dinner? What should I do? God doesn't always tell us exactly what to do, but he does promise to help. God has given us parents, teachers, coaches, and the Bible. These help us make right choices.

God wants you to ask him for help because he loves you and wants what is best for you!

***Thank you, heavenly Father, for helping me wherever I go. Help me to know your voice.***

# Go through It!

*"When you pass through the waters, I will be with you; and through the rivers, they shall not overwhelm you; when you walk through fire you shall not be burned, and the flame shall not consume you."*

ISAIAH 43:2 NRSV

Do you know that story about the family that went on a bear hunt? All kinds of things got in their way: squishy mud, long grass, a snowstorm, a forest, a big river. The story says, "You can't go over it; you can't go under it; oh no, you've got to go through it!"

Sometimes we have to go through things that make us afraid. It might be your first day at a new school, or trying out for a sports team, eating a new kind of food, or sleeping through a big storm. God promises to be with you through all of these.

*Lord, help me to have courage and to go through things that I am afraid of, knowing that you are with me every step of the way.*

54

# Consider His Hand

*"Look at the new thing I am going to do.
It is already happening. Don't you see it?
I will make a road in the desert.
I will make rivers in the dry land."*

ISAIAH 43:19 ICB

Trail walks can be fun and interesting. You go through lots of bushes and trees. Did you know that other people had to make those trails? They had to find a good path, clear away the bushes, and sometimes build little bridges across the rivers.

God is like our trail maker. The Bible says that he goes before us in life. That means he knows what is going to happen, and he gets things ready for us.

***Lord, I can't even count all the ways
you've helped me and kept me going.
Thank you for thinking about me all the time!***

# In the Morning

*I wake up early in the morning and cry out.
I trust your word.*
PSALM 119:147 ICB

What is the first thing you like to do in the morning? Do you head to the kitchen for breakfast, do you play on a device, or do you get dressed straight away? The writer of this Bible verse thought that it was a good thing to wake up and think about God. How do you think you could do that?

You might have a Bible or story books about God; you might have some church songs you could listen to. Maybe you just wake up and say, "Hello, Jesus, thank you for today." You can trust that he will be listening.

**Help me, Jesus, to start every day with you.**
**Thank you that you are with me all the time.**

# Be with Friends

*"My soul is overwhelmed with sorrow to the point of death. Stay here and keep watch with me."*
MATTHEW 26:38 NIV

This verse was written about the night Jesus was taken to jail. It tells us how Jesus felt. He was actually sad. He understands how that feels. He won't be disappointed if you have trouble putting on a smile. He knows what it is like.

Jesus brought three close friends to the garden to pray that night. None of us are meant to be alone. If even Jesus needed the people he loved, so do we.

*Jesus, you know what it is like to be sad. Thank you that you understand me. Thank you for showing me that I need friends, just like you did.*

# A Guarded Heart

*Above all else, guard your heart,*
*for everything you do flows from it.*
PROVERBS 4:23 NIV

Picture the biggest, coolest, most beautiful castle that you can imagine. Does it have people inside it? Does it have lovely gardens and bridges and lots of rooms? Are there guards standing outside of it? There should be! Guards help to keep the castle safe from enemies.

Your heart is just like that awesome castle. God wants you to protect it, so his Word says to guard it! This means to be careful not to let the wrongs things get in.

**Lord, help me guard my heart.**
**Show me what things are good,**
**and protect me from the wrong things.**

# Hesitant

*"The Father gives me the people who are mine. Every one of them will come to me, and I will always accept them."*

JOHN 6:37 ICB

God's arms are always open to us, but sometimes we are afraid to go to him. We don't always feel like we deserve to have his love, and we are embarrassed by our sins. We think maybe he will turn away from us.

But God says we are always welcome. There is nothing we could do that would cause him to reject us. Nothing can keep us from his love.

***Thank you, Jesus, for always loving me and drawing me closer to you. I am thankful that you accept me for all that I am.***

# Bragging

*"If a person brags, he should brag only about the Lord." It is not the one who says he is good who is accepted but the one that the Lord thinks is good.*

2 CORINTHIANS 10:17-18 ICB

It's okay to want to be noticed for the good things you do, but there are times when we need to think about others before we show off. What does it feel like when someone says that they are the best at throwing a ball, or drawing a picture, or doing math?

God looks at the heart, and he wants us to be good and kind to everyone. Instead of bragging about yourself, tell others about how amazing they are. This is the kind of heart that God thinks is good.

*Lord, thank you that I am good at a lot of things, but thank you that it is more important to be kind and show love to others. Help me to brag only about your goodness!*

# Gift of Peace

*"I am leaving you with a gift—peace of mind and heart. And the peace I give is a gift the world cannot give. So don't be troubled or afraid."*

JOHN 14:27 NLT

Everybody likes to get presents! Can you think of a time when you got a gift that you really, really wanted? Or a gift that you had never had before?

Jesus describes peace as a gift like this. It's something that only he can give, not something that anyone in this world could wrap up for you. It's one of the best gifts, because peace helps us to be calm when things are tough. Open up his gift of peace, today.

***Jesus, thank you for giving me the gift of peace. When things get hard, help me to remember that I don't have to be afraid because you are with me.***

# Growing in God

*This is my prayer for you: that your love will grow more and more; that you will have knowledge and understanding with your love; that you will see the difference between good and bad and choose the good.*

PHILIPPIANS 1:9-10 ICB

You are growing every single day! There are probably a lot of people, especially your parents, that talk about how big you are getting, and how smart you are becoming.

When you stick close to Jesus, you grow more and more in his love. You will understand more about the Bible and who Jesus is as time goes on. Make sure that you keep learning about God because it will help you to choose the best things for your life.

*Lord, I want to know more about you. Help me to understand you more, and most of all, to love you more.*

# Join Together

*May God, who gives this patience and encouragement, help you live in complete harmony with each other, as is fitting for followers of Christ Jesus. Then all of you can join together with one voice, giving praise and glory to God, the Father of our Lord Jesus Christ.*

ROMANS 15:5-6 NLT

When a choir comes together to sing, they don't all sing the same tune, they sing different parts called harmonies. They sing different notes, but all the notes sound beautiful together.

This is how Jesus wants us to live with other people: with our friends, our family, and our church. Everyone is a little bit different, but he wants us to use those differences to sound good together. That means that he wants us to love each other, to be ourselves, and to all get along!

**Lord, help me to be kind to everyone around me, and to remember that everyone is special. Thank you that together we can make beautiful music for you.**

# Never Alone

*Can anything separate us from the love Christ has for us? Can troubles or problems or sufferings? If we have no food or clothes, if we are in danger, or even if death comes—can any of these things separate us from Christ's love?*

ROMANS 8:35 ICB

Have you ever noticed how much the Bible talks about love? Love is so important that God says it's the whole reason that he created us. When you feel that nobody loves you, tell yourself, "I am not alone! Nothing can separate me from the love of Christ! I am strong in him!"

Troubles will come, but we always have the love of God to lean on. We can face more than we ever knew because he fights our battles with us.

*Lord, thank you for loving me through everything. When life seems hard, I will remember that nothing can separate me from your love.*

# Think Lovely Things

*Continue to think about the things that are good and worthy of praise. Think about the things that are true and honorable and right and pure and beautiful and respected.*

PHILIPPIANS 4:8 ICB

Have you ever woken up from a bad dream? Sometimes yucky thoughts can get into our heads and it can be a little scary. Well, the words of the Bible tell us that there is something that we can do about bad thoughts. We can practice thinking about good things.

Try it now. Think of something that makes you laugh, something that makes you feel happy. Think of something that makes you proud, and something that you are good at. Think of the things that you are thankful for in your life. See? You can think good thoughts!

*Lord, when bad thoughts or pictures come into my mind, please remind me of all the lovely and right things that I can think about.*

65

# Our Rock

*There isn't anyone holy like the LORD.*
*There isn't anyone except him.*
*There isn't any Rock like our God.*

1 SAMUEL 2:2 NIRV

What is the biggest rock that you have seen? Did you try to pick it up? How heavy do you think it was? Rocks are strong and secure and the biggest ones are almost impossible to move.

When we start to worry, or become afraid, think about God like a rock. No matter what it is we are going through, he won't move. You can trust him!

*God, I am so thankful that you are my rock and my strength. I pray that I would remember to turn to you first in all that I do.*

# MARCH

The LORD is holy and kind.
Our God is full of tender love.

PSALM 116:5 NIRV

# Mighty God

*Lord and King, you have reached out your great and powerful arm. You have made the heavens and the earth. Nothing is too hard for you.*

JEREMIAH 32:17 NIRV

When you come home from shopping with a parent they might get you to help by bringing in some of the bags. Sometimes those bags can get heavy, especially when there is a big bottle of milk or juice inside of it. You might remember a time when you couldn't hold the bag and had to put it on the ground.

We have times when things are too hard, but the Bible says that nothing is ever too hard for God. Nothing! He can handle everything. He power is so great that he created everything. What a mighty God!

**Lord, thank you for making the heavens and the earth. I know that nothing is too hard for you.**

# No Greater Love

*This is how we know what real love is: Jesus gave his life for us. So we should give our lives for our brothers.*
1 John 3:16 ICB

There isn't a better example of love than Jesus Christ. He gave up his entire life for love. He left the beautiful heavens and came down to earth so you could spend forever with him. He did what was best for you!

While many of us won't actually have to die for another person, there are plenty of ways to show our love for others. The best way to show love is to think about what is best for the other person, just like Jesus did for you.

*Jesus, thank you for giving up your life in heaven and coming to earth to rescue me from sin. Help me to love others the way you love me.*

# Courage

*"Remember that I commanded you to be strong and brave. So don't be afraid. The Lord your God will be with you everywhere you go."*

JOSHUA 1:9 ICB

What does it feel like to stand up in front of the class to read something out loud, or talk about a project you just finished? Do you get a little nervous? Do you get really nervous? Don't worry, most people are afraid of talking to groups of people.

Maybe the next time you are facing something that makes you nervous, you can remember that you have a big strong God standing next to you. He can give you the courage to do anything. So, take a deep breath and relax! God is on your side.

*God, I pray that you will help me overcome my fears by remembering that you are with me always. Thank you for your strength.*

# Share the Love

*Does your life in Christ give you strength? Does his love comfort you? Do we share together in the Spirit? Do you have mercy and kindness? If so, make me very happy by having the same thoughts, sharing the same love, and having one mind and purpose.*

PHILIPPIANS 2:1-2 ICB

Some schools have a special bench that you can go sit on when you are feeling lonely and need some friends. It's called a buddy bench. If you see someone sitting on that bench, you can go up and ask them if they want to play with you. Why is this such a good idea? Because everybody knows that it's no fun to be alone!

Jesus wants us to get along with others. It lets others know that you are full of his love. Can you make an effort to get along with people today?

**Lord, help me to be an awesome friend so I can share your love with others.**

# Stay Away from Evil

*You who love the LORD, hate evil!*
*He protects the lives of his godly people*
*and rescues them from the power of the wicked.*
PSALM 97:10 NLT

What's your favorite movie? Most movies have some kind of good and evil in them. The bad guys usually try to do mean things and destroy everything, but the good guys win in the end.

God asks us to hate evil because he wants us to stay away from things that are wrong. When you notice things that are evil, be sure to stay away from those things. But you don't have to be afraid of evil. God says when you love him, he rescues you!

**Lord, thank you for guarding me from evil. I pray for those who are troubled today, that they may see your light.**

# Everlasting Love

*"I have loved you with a love that lasts forever.*
*I have kept on loving you*
*with a kindness that never fails."*
JEREMIAH 31:3 NIRV

Sometimes we think about ourselves and wonder why God would love us. Maybe we have done something wrong, or can't seem to get anything right. It doesn't matter. God says he loves us—always!

Isn't it amazing that God loves us this way? Who else could love like that? Think about God's love because it is for you today, tomorrow, and forever.

*Father, thank you for loving me no matter what.*
*May your love for me be a reminder to love*
*others well.*

# Keep Calm

*Don't become mad quickly
because getting angry is foolish.*
ECCLESIASTES 7:9 ICB

Your brother pulls your hair and it makes you want to scream. You get all the answers wrong at school and are frustrated. A friend treats you unfairly and anger bubbles up inside. One more thing and you'll snap!

If there is one thing worse than anger, it's feeling stupid. The Bible says that if we give in to that quick burst of anger, we are foolish. The power of the Holy Spirit can keep you calm and he will help you when you ask.

*Lord, help me when I am angry.
I pray others would see patience
in me as I respond in a good way
to frustrating situations.*

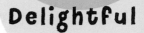

# Delightful

*The Lord is pleased with his people.*
*He saves those who are not proud.*

PSALM 149:4 ICB

The Lord is pleased with you! He is delighted by you. He is so happy thinking about you. He tells us this in his Word. He loves the fact that you were even born!

He created you to have a relationship with him, and he gets a lot of joy out of it.

Tuck it away in your heart: there is one who loves you more than anything, and  he loves spending time with you.

*Father, it makes me smile to know that you delight in your people. Thank you for loving me like this!*

# Don't Panic

*So don't worry, because I am with you.*
*Don't be afraid, because I am your God.*
*I will make you strong and will help you.*
*I will support you with my right hand that saves you.*
ISAIAH 41:10 ICB

Is there something you are worried about, making it hard for you to feel okay about things? The Lord tells us we don't need to be afraid. He will strengthen us and help us. He holds us in his hands.

Think of a steep path that goes around and up a huge cliff. Imagine yourself walking on it. You might think that you could fall. Now picture God standing right next to you, holding you up. He's not going to let you fall, and he'll give you strength to take another step. It's his promise to you!

**Lord, I don't have to be afraid because you are holding me, keeping me safe and protected from whatever life may throw my way.**

# Eternal Gift

*The Lord's love
for those who have respect for him
lasts for ever and ever.
Their children's children will know
that he always does what is right.
He always loves those who keep his covenant.
He always does what is right for those who remember
to obey his commands.*

PSALM 103:17-18 NIRV

What are your grandparents like? Do you call them Grandma, Grandpa, Nana, or Poppa? Maybe you have other great names for them. Grandparents remind us that the love of a family goes on and on. They love your parents, and they love you.

That's just like God—he loves and loves and keeps on loving. The best thing that you can do is love him back. This makes love go on forever!

*Father, I am amazed by your love
and how you give it freely.
Help me to love you, too, always.*

# Example of Love

"I give you a new command. Love one another.
You must love one another, just as I have loved you.
If you love one another, everyone will know
you are my disciples."

JOHN 13:34-35 NIRV

How do you know when people are nice? They smile, share, and say kind things. Nice people feel good to be around. Nice people seem to have a lot of friends.

Jesus said that we can show his love by loving one another. People can know that there is something wonderful about you and about Jesus just by watching how you treat other people! Isn't that cool? We don't have to say anything; Jesus just asks us to love one another!

*Lord, open my eyes to see where I can be an example of your love today. Let others see you in me in everything I say and do.*

# Hope in His Word

*You are my hiding place and my shield;*
*I hope in your word.*
PSALM 119:114 NCV

Hope means looking forward to something and getting excited about what is coming. Have you ever felt that way about reading the Bible?

God protects us and wants what is best for us, so he gave us the Bible full of promises. We can always go to it if we start to wonder about things or want strength or courage or love—because God and his truth are there.

*Father, thank you for giving us the Bible. I pray that I would find hope and peace in your Word.*

# Not a Quitter

*Give thanks to the LORD, for he is good*
*his love endures forever.*
1 CHRONICLES 16:34 NIV

What is your favorite board game? Have you ever been playing a game that someone else is winning and you just want to quit?

God never feels like quitting on us. Isn't that amazing? He doesn't sit on his throne with a big frown, mad at us for all of our mistakes. He is not surprised by anything we do. He just loves us, and he wants to help us through. He wants us to know we are not alone.

*Father, thank you for your strong love*
*that helps me through everything.*
*Help me remember your love when*
*I feel lost or lonely. I know you*
*will never quit on me.*

# The Thrill of the Hunt

*Whoever pursues righteousness and kindness will find life and honor.*

PROVERBS 21:21 NRSV

Do you like treasure hunts? Trying to find treats, money, or candy is pretty exciting! This is what it means to pursue something—to go looking and looking until you find it!

If we want to live a life that really means something, we must pursue God. We must always be looking for him and looking for all that is good and true. It's like finding the best, golden Easter egg, but it's better because we have found a life in heaven where treasures are everywhere!

**Lord, I pray for your help in finding real life in you. Keep me on your path as I continue my hunt.**

# Rain to Grow

*Rejoice in the Lord your God!*
*For the rain he sends demonstrates his faithfulness.*
*Once more the autumn rains will come,*
*as well as the rains of spring.*
JOEL 2:23 NLT

Do you know what plants look like when they haven't had any water? They go all brown and droopy. Sometimes we feel like a brown and droopy plant. We can get sad and tired and not feel very joyful.

God cares enough for us to help bring us closer to him. He tells us hopeful things that can be just like water for a dried out tree. He wants to see us doing great things, like the way a tree begins making fruit when it is watered. God will continue to give us what we need to grow.

**Lord, thank you for protecting me from drying out. You give me everything I need to grow and to be joyful.**

# Rest Easy

*Praise the Lord, day by day.*
*God our Savior helps us.*
PSALM 68:19 ICB

Have you ever had so many things in your school bag that it became really hard to carry? What does it feel like when a friend or parent takes that bag off you and carries it for you? It's a relief, right?

Sometimes our hearts feel like they have too much to carry. We are afraid, sad, or lonely. The Bible says that Jesus comes and takes that heaviness away. What a relief to know he is ready to do that whenever we ask him to!

**Lord, thank you for being strong enough to carry the things that make my heart heavy. I gladly give them to you!**

# He Fights for You

*In all these things we are more than conquerors through him who loved us.*
ROMANS 8:37 NIV

Imagine you are fighting a battle with all your might. There are swords flying and people falling but then all of a sudden you see a fearless leader at the front slaying dragons right and left. Anyone who dares attack him loses badly because he has so much skill and power. That leader is Jesus and he fights for you!

Jesus fills us with his strength and courage to face everything that comes our way. He is on our side, and nothing can keep us down. Nothing can defeat us. Nothing is too hard for Jesus.

**Father, thank you for fighting my battles for me. I pray I would turn to you each time I need help.**

# Faithful without Fail

*Let us hold firmly to the hope that we have confessed.
We can trust God to do what he promised.*

HEBREWS 10:23 ICB

It can be disappointing when we have plans and then for some reason they don't happen. Maybe your friend couldn't come over to your house because they got sick, or your family was planning to go to the beach and it started to rain. Sometimes people just don't show up when they said they would!

God is not like any of these situations. The Bible says that he is faithful which means that he always, always, always does what he has promised. You can trust in him.

*Lord, I pray I'd always remember you and the promises you have made. My hope is in you.*

# His Love Song

*"The Lord your God is with you.
The mighty One will save you.
The Lord will be happy with you.
You will rest in his love.
He will sing and be joyful about you."*

ZEPHANIAH 3:17 ICB

One of the most popular reasons people buy puppies is so that there is always someone excited to see them when they get home. A puppy forgives quickly and loves to spend as much time with its owner as possible.

Smile! The Lord loves you with more excitement than a puppy! He gets so much joy from his relationship with you that he sings about it!

***Lord, I pray I would listen for your song as I remember how much you love me!***

# Intimate Friendship

*The grace of the Lord Jesus Christ, the love of God,
and the fellowship of the Holy Spirit be with you all.*
2 CORINTHIANS 13:14 ICB

What do you like to do with your friends? Do you invite them to your parties? Play games with them? Do you like talking about interesting things with them?

God wants to be your friend! There is a special friendship between God, Jesus, and the Holy Spirit and they want you to join in this friendship. The very best way to be a good friend of God is to talk to him. You don't see God, but he sees you and he cares about everything you have to say!

*Lord, you consider me a friend,
and I think that's great. Help me
to be a good friend to you by talking
and listening to you.*

# Good News

*Give thanks to the LORD and proclaim his greatness.*
*Let the whole world know what he has done.*
*Sing to him; yes, sing his praises.*
*Tell everyone about his wonderful deeds.*
*Exult in his holy name;*
*rejoice, you who worship the LORD.*

1 CHRONICLES 16:8-10 NLT

How do you know when something really great has happened—like you're getting a new baby brother or sister, or your favorite sports team is winning a game? Your parents probably tell you the great news, or sometimes you read it or see it on your computer.

God is the picture of everything good. He has done so many wonderful things for us. Let's tell others about the good things he has done!

**Lord, thank you for all that you've done for me. Help me to share your good news with others.**

# The Best Outfit

*You are God's chosen people. You are holy and dearly loved. So put on tender mercy and kindness as if they were your clothes. Don't be proud. Be gentle and patient.*
COLOSSIANS 3:12 NIRV

What is your favorite thing to wear? Is it a certain jacket, or sports shirt? Maybe you enjoy dressing up in a costume, or maybe you just like wearing your pajamas!

The Bible talks about putting on clothes of kindness and gentleness and patience. What would that look like? We would make a decision to be a kind, gentle, loving person. When we remember to be kind, humble, and gentle we will always feel like we are wearing our best clothes.

**Father, help me to remember to dress properly today, putting on good things like kindness, patience, love, and gentleness.**

# Growing Stronger

*Christ will live in your hearts because you believe in him. And I pray that your love will have deep roots. I pray that it will have a strong foundation. May you have power together with all the Lord's holy people to understand Christ's love. May you know how wide and long and high and deep it is. And may you know his love, even though it can't be known completely. Then you will be filled with everything God has for you.*

EPHESIANS 3:17-19 NIRV

The best trees to climb are the big ones because they have a lot of really strong branches. The biggest, strongest trees have roots that have grown so deep into the ground that they are almost as big as the tree itself!

Trusting the promises of God is kind of like a growing tree. As you get to know Jesus, your relationship with him grows stronger. As his Holy Spirit fills you, your love grows. As your love grows, your faith will grow, and in him you will do great things.

**Heavenly Father, help me to grow stronger and stronger in you by understanding more and more of your love.**

# Ask Confidently

*Let us come boldly to the very throne of God and stay there to receive his mercy and to find grace to help us in our times of need.*

HEBREWS 4:16 TLB

When you don't know how to do something at school, what do you do? You can't just sit there and wait for someone to tell you. You have to go find somebody who knows and ask them to help you. Teachers love it when you tell them that you don't quite understand.

God is the same! It gives him joy to be able to help you when you need it, because he loves you and he wants what is best for you. Be brave; ask him for help!

***Lord, thank you for wanting to help me.***
***I know I can come to you with all my needs.***

91

# Wildest Dreams

*God is able to do far more than we could ever ask for or imagine. He does everything by his power that is working in us. Give him glory in the church and in Christ Jesus. Give him glory through all time and for ever and ever. Amen.*

EPHESIANS 3:20-21 NIRV

Do you know what boats need to go really fast? They either need a big motor or they need really strong wind!

There are a lot of things that you might want to do when you get older—like become a doctor, or a mechanic, or a really good chef! The Bible verse says that God can do even greater things for you than you can dream of right now. God is just like that big motor or a really strong wind. He will keep you going strong and fast!

**Father, thank you that I'm able to do so much more with you than I ever could on my own.**

# Victory over Struggles

*How we thank God for all of this! It is he who makes us victorious through Jesus Christ our Lord!*
1 Corinthians 15:57 TLB

Sometimes it is really hard to lose a game because we know how good it feels to win. Everybody likes to win. Well, guess what? When we know Jesus, we know we are on the winning side!

It doesn't matter what is going on around you, Jesus will bring every good thing that you need. Strength, joy, bravery, love. In the end, we will get to be with him and everyone who loves him in heaven. We win!

**Jesus, thank you that I am on your winning side. I am excited for all the good things you have for my life!**

# Effortlessly Good

*The Lord is good. His faithful love continues forever.*
*It will last for all time to come.*
PSALM 100:5 NIRV

Have you ever watched a clock hand tick around and around, or heard it making that tick-tock noise? On and on it goes. A clock is a circle because it never ends, just like time never ends!

God is the one who made that time, and his love is like that clock! It keeps going around and around, through all the times before us and it will keep going through all the times ahead of us. He is always good, and his love lasts forever.

**Father, I pray I would remember your everlasting love and know that it is for everyone.**

# Stand Your Ground

*Remain strong in the faith. Don't let anything move you. Always give yourselves completely to the work of the Lord. Because you belong to the Lord, you know that your work is not worthless.*

1 CORINTHIANS 15:58 NIRV

Do your parents give you jobs around the house? They might ask you to take the trash outside, or to help clear the dishes, or to set the table. There might be some gross jobs like cleaning the toilets.

What if these jobs weren't done? We would have a house full of trash, dishes with old food stuck on them, and dirty toilets! God wants us to help our parents. Everybody has to work! God notices all the hard work you do, and he will reward you for doing it.

**Lord, help me to be joyful about the jobs that my parents ask me to do. Help me to remember that it makes you happy when I help others.**

# You Can Always Pray

*First, I tell you to pray for all people. Ask God for the things people need, and be thankful to him. You should pray for kings and for all who have authority. Pray for the leaders so that we can have quiet and peaceful lives—lives full of worship and respect for God.*

1 TIMOTHY 2:1-2 NLT

Do you ever wonder what to pray about? It can be hard to think of things. Well, the Bible says that you can start with praying for people. You could ask God to bring happiness to children in other countries, or to help kids at school to be brave. You can pray for everyone you know, like your teachers, people at church, and your own family.

We should even pray for our country's leaders so they can lead us better. If you think of people, you will have a lot to pray for!

**Father, thank you for listening to me when I pray. Help me to think of people that need my prayer, and remind me to pray each day.**

# Your Thought Life

*Letting your sinful nature control your mind leads to death. But letting the Spirit control your mind leads to life and peace.*

ROMANS 8:6 NLT

Your parents drive a car using a steering wheel. They control which way the car goes by turning their hands to the left or to the right. Did you know you can control your mind like this? You decide what to think!

The thoughts in your mind are very powerful. The actions you take come from the thoughts you think, so good thoughts lead to good actions. Bad thoughts lead to bad actions. Be careful what you think about, and make sure those things honor God.

**Father, please fill me with more of your Holy Spirit today so I can control my mind and choose to be more peaceful.**

# Things You Don't Know

*"I made the earth. I formed it. And I set it in place.
The LORD is my name. Call out to me. I will answer you.
I will tell you great things you do not know. And unless
I do, you wouldn't be able to find out about them."*

JEREMIAH 33:2-3 NIRV

Have you ever wondered how the ocean got so deep, or why the sky is blue? Do you know why some trees grow tall and others stay small? The earth is amazing! God created this earth, so he knows exactly how it all works.

God can help you understand some of the things that you don't know. He wants you to understand more about life, about the earth, about the kind of person he has made you. He says that he will answer your questions, so ask!

*Father, you're an awesome creator. I have
so many questions and I pray that you
would show me the answers.*

# APRIL

Even though you are bad, you know
how to give good gifts to your children.
So surely your heavenly Father will give
good things to those who ask him.

MATTHEW 7:11 NIRV

# Made Whole

*We pray that God himself, the God of peace, will make you pure, belonging only to him. We pray that your whole self—spirit, soul, and body—will be kept safe and be without wrong when our Lord Jesus Christ comes.*

1 THESSALONIANS 5:23 ICB

Do you ever wish you could be in two places at one time? Maybe you have to choose between birthday parties, or whether you will go with Mom or Dad. You might need to finish your homework, but you also really want to play. We can only be in one place at a time, right? That's how our body, mind, and feelings work—all together.

Jesus came to make all things about us right—our body, our mind, and our feelings. He wants to keep our whole selves safe and good.

*Jesus, thank you that you care that I have a healthy body, a healthy mind, and healthy feelings. Heal all of these in me, in your name.*

100

# Sit Down

"There is only one thing worth being concerned
about. Mary has discovered it,
and it will not be taken away from her."

LUKE 10:42 NLT

Moms can be really busy people, can't they? They
have a lot to do. They work, they take care of children,
they clean, they cook. Do you sometimes wish your
mom would just stop and sit down with you?

Mary and Martha were sisters in the Bible, and
Martha had a lot of things to do, like a busy mom.
Mary might have had a lot to do as well, but one
time she chose to sit down with Jesus and just listen
to him. Jesus thought this was more important than
doing all that work, don't you?

*Jesus, help me to be like Mary and realize
just how important it is to spend time
listening to you.*

# Light of Love

*You are chosen people. You are the King's priests. You are a holy nation. You are a nation that belongs to God alone. God chose you to tell about the wonderful things he has done. He called you out of darkness into his wonderful light.*

1 Peter 2:9 ICB

What is it like when you first turn out the light at night? It can be pretty dark if you don't have any kind of light. Do you leave a light on in another room so that you can see just a little bit? It feels better to be able to see, doesn't it?

Before we knew Jesus, we were like people without a light, afraid of the dark. Now life is bright! Jesus is our lamp that gives us courage, strength, and peace.

**Lord, thank you that our darkness has gone. I want to live only in the light of your love.**

# Superhero

*This is what the LORD says.*
*He created you, people of Jacob;*
*he formed you, people of Israel.*
*He says, "Don't be afraid, because I have saved you.*
*I have called you by name, and you are mine."*

ISAIAH 43:1 NCV

Who is your favorite superhero? Is it Superman, Batman, Spiderman or Wonder woman? Maybe it is someone else. A superhero is awesome because they can hear when people need help and they are fast and strong. They seem to always save people from trouble.

Jesus is the best superhero. He says not to be afraid because he has rescued you from the very worst thing; he has rescued you from death. You never have to be afraid because he has given you eternal life in heaven.

***Lord, I'm so glad I belong to you. Thank you for saving me from death. You're my best superhero!***

# Stepping Out

*God did not give us a spirit that makes us afraid. He gave us a spirit of power and love and self-control.*
2 TIMOTHY 1:7 ICB

When Jesus left earth to go to heaven, he sent his Holy Spirit. We can't see the Holy Spirit, but we can ask him to help us all the time.

You can know that the Holy Spirit has helped you when you realize that you are not afraid anymore, or when you have a lot of strength or love. You know he is helping you when you seem to be doing good things a lot. Are you letting the Holy Spirit help you, today?

**Holy Spirit, thank you that you walk with me every day. Let me remember to ask you for help.**

# Waiting and Praying

*Rejoice in our confident hope. Be patient in trouble, and keep on praying.*
ROMANS 12:12 NLT

Have you ever gone to an amusement park and had to wait in line for a really long time to get on a ride? Maybe you have been to a movie and had to wait a while before it started. It can be hard to wait!

God has promised that one day he will make everything right on earth again. We will have a new heaven and a new earth and there will be no more trouble. But we have to wait! Can you wait patiently? The Bible says to be patient and to keep on praying, because it will happen!

*Lord, thank you that you plan great things for our lives and for this world. Help me to keep praying, knowing that you are planning it just right.*

# Follow His Rules

*When I learned that your laws are fair,
I praised you with an honest heart.*
PSALM 119:7 ICB

Think about driving in a car without any stop lights or lines. Car wouldn't know what side of the road to go on, and nobody would stop to wait for other cars. It would be a mess, and there would be a lot of accidents!

Jesus gives us really good rules. They are rules that will be helpful for making decisions, and rules that keep us and others safe. Look in the Bible for his rules and decide to follow him! He knows what is best for us.

**Father, I choose you! Help me to live by your rules so that I can stay safe and happy.**

# No Grudges

*Be kind to each other, tenderhearted,
forgiving one another, just as God has forgiven you
because you belong to Christ.*
EPHESIANS 4:32 TLB

Have you ever seen what happens to butter when you leave it in the warm air? Have you ever seen what happens to cheese? Well, the butter melts, and the cheese gets really hard.

Did you know that Jesus wants us to be soft, like that butter? When someone hurts you, you feel like getting mad and doing something back to them. But forgiving someone means you walk away and love them anyway! It is hard, but remember that this is what Jesus did for all of us.

*Lord, thank you for forgiving me of all the wrong things I do. Help me to be soft toward others and to forgive them like you do.*

# Much Stronger

*Be strong in the Lord and in his mighty power.*
EPHESIANS 6:10 NIV

Do you know how much power and strength you have? It doesn't feel like it when you are young and smaller than others, but the power comes from Jesus, not from you. It's called the Holy Spirit and he's ready to give you his strength when you don't have any of your own.

God is mighty, and he gladly shares his strength with us so we can face anything like a strong Olympic athlete or a hero!

**Lord, I'm in awe of your power and might. I'm so thankful that you make me strong.**

# Working with Joy

*In all the work you are doing, work the best you can.*
*Work as if you were working for the Lord, not for men.*
*Remember that you will receive your reward from*
*the Lord, which he promised to his people. You are*
*serving the Lord Christ.*

COLOSSIANS 3:23-24 ICB

Sometimes we have to work, like doing homework or jobs that your parents ask you to do. Sometime these jobs can be fun, and sometimes they can be boring! The Bible says to remember that we do our jobs for God, not just for the teacher or our parents.

God loves us so much and we are promised a reward better than anything we can imagine if we work hard. If you think about your work like this, you'll be surprised at how much it helps.

**Lord, I want to serve you. I'm excited to receive my reward from you. Help me to work with my whole heart, knowing I'm pleasing you.**

# The Rock

*Trust in the LORD always,*
*for the LORD GOD is the eternal Rock.*
ISAIAH 26:4 NLT

What do you think of when you think of a rock? Do you think of words like solid, strong, and firm? God is like a rock—he is solid and dependable. He is more than strong enough for you.

It's easy to trust someone who is solid, right? You know they will always be there for you. That's our God! Smile. Relax. God will never let you down.

**Lord, thank you for being my rock. I cannot imagine life without you. I know that you are always strong enough for me.**

# Don't Get Lost!

*May the Lord lead your hearts into God's love and Christ's patience.*

2 THESSALONIANS 3:5 NCV

Have you ever been lost in a store and couldn't find your parents? It can be pretty scary. All it takes is to walk in a different direction or hide behind a bench and suddenly you don't know where your family has gone!

We have to follow Jesus closely. He always knows where we are, but we need to make sure we know where he is and where he wants us to go. Follow him by remembering to love him in everything that you do.

*Lord, thank you for leading me on the path you want for me. I pray I'd turn to you each time I'm tempted to go the wrong way.*

# Great Bonus

*You must hold on, so you can do what God wants and receive what he has promised.*
HEBREWS 10:36 ICB

Do you like swings? How high can you go? What would happen if you let go of the ropes on the swing? You would fall! It's important that we hold on because this is what helps us go higher.

The Bible says that we have to hold on to God like this. That means that we keep following him all the days of our life. He has promised us a life in heaven, so don't ever let go of him.

**Lord, thank you for your promises. I can't wait to receive your gift of eternal life!**

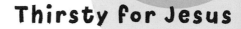

# Thirsty for Jesus

*God, you are my God.*
*I want to follow you.*
*My whole being thirsts for you,*
*like a man in a dry, empty land where*
*there is no water.*

PSALM 63:1 ICB

Have you seen what a desert looks like? It's a very hot place full of sand with no water around. Not many things can live in a desert. What would it be like to be in a hot, empty desert without water?

When we think of God as the most important thing in our life, we will want to be with him in the same way that you would want water in a desert. It's good to want to know more about God and to want to be closer to him.

**Father, I want to be closer to you. Thank you that you let me get to know you better each day.**

# You Can't Hide!

*Nothing in all the world can be hidden from God. Everything is clear and lies open before him. And to him we must explain the way we have lived.*

HEBREWS 4:13 ICB

We can't hide anything from God. That might sometimes be scary because we have little secrets we would rather keep hidden. You should feel safe knowing that God sees and knows everything and he still loves you!

There is nothing we can do to make him stop loving us. God knows when we've messed up and he takes us by the hand and loves us anyway. Praise God!

*Lord, thank you for knowing me so well. You know where I make mistakes and you love me anyway.*

# Zoom In

*From heaven the LORD looks down*
*and sees everyone.*
*From his throne he watches*
*all those who live on the earth.*
*He creates the hearts of all people.*
*He is aware of everything they do.*

PSALM 33:13-15 NIRV

When you look at maps on a computer, you can usually see whole countries, cities, and towns. It is cool to see things from so high up. You can see where the rivers, streets, buildings, and farms are.

God can see us from a distance, but he can also zoom in and see every single person. He can zoom in even more to see your heart and mind, and know everything that goes on inside of you. He doesn't just see you, he understands you, because he made you.

**Thank you for watching over me, Lord. I know that you love me, because you made me.**

115

# Search and Find

*You will also begin to search again for Jehovah your God, and you will find him when you search for him with all your heart and soul.*

DEUTERONOMY 4:29 TLB

God doesn't hide from us. He doesn't make it difficult for us to find him. We simply have to look for him and he will show himself to us.

It might be hard to find something that you can't see, but God can be found in the Bible, when you are praying, and when other people talk about him. He can be found when you need to feel safe or loved. He can be found anywhere that you want to find truth.

**Father, thank you for making it so easy to find your love. Show yourself to me, today.**

116

# A Beautiful Sound

*To choose life is to love the LORD your God, obey him, and stay close to him. He is your life, and he will let you live many years in the land, the land he promised to give your ancestors Abraham, Isaac, and Jacob.*
DEUTERONOMY 30:20 NCV

Do your parents still tell you to stay close to them when you cross the road? Maybe they make you hold their hand. The reason they do this is because they want to protect you from the dangers of a busy road. They want to keep you safe.

God wants to keep you safe, too. That's why he says to stay close to him. He wants you to live a long happy life, just like he has promised other friends of his, like Abraham, Isaac, and Jacob.

**Father, thank you for keeping me safe. Help me to stay close by your side so that I can live a great life.**

# Living Abundantly

*The thief comes only to steal and kill and destroy;*
*I have come that they may have life,*
*and have it to the full.*
JOHN 10:10 NIV

In Bible times, shepherds used to have to keep careful watch over their sheep because wolves could attack, or thieves could try to steal the sheep away.

Jesus says that he is like a good shepherd who protects his sheep from being hurt. Jesus gives his friends life, not death, and he wants to give us an awesome life.

*Lord, thank you that you rescue me and that you give me the chance for a wonderful life.*

# Loved First

*We love because he first loved us.*
1 John 4:19 esv

When you have had a fight with your brother, sister, or friend, someone has to say sorry first. It is hard to the be one to apologize, but it always helps the other person feel better, and usually it helps them say sorry too.

This is kind of how it works with God. He loved you first. He chose to create you and to give you life. He knows you inside-out, and he loves every part of you. When you know how much he loves you, it makes you want to love just the same. That's how loving first works!

**Father, thank you for loving me first. Help me to be the kind of person that shows love to others first.**

# Good not Gross

*Taste and see that the Lord is good.*
*Oh, the joys of those who take refuge in him!*
PSALM 34:8 NLT

How do you know when food is good or when it's gross? You taste it! You put something in your mouth and very quickly you know whether you like it or not. Isn't it great when what you put in your mouth is delicious?

We know that God is good because we like what he does for us. When we feel loved, cared for, and protected, we know that this is God. Be happy today, knowing things from God are not gross but are really, really good!

*Lord, thank you for your goodness. Thank you that I can taste and see your goodness all around me.*

# Teach Me

*Guide me in your truth. Teach me.*
*You are God my Savior.*
*I put my hope in you all day long.*
PSALM 25:5 NIRV

Think of what your favorite teacher is like. Kind? Funny? Maybe your favorite teacher knows how to explain things really well. A good teacher cares about you learning things right. They are probably kind, but they have rules too.

Jesus is the best teacher. He wants you to learn his truth, so he will make sure to teach you. He is a kind teacher, a fair teacher, and probably even a funny teacher! Remember that you can trust him to show you the right way.

**Lord, I'm putting my hope and trust in you.**
**Guide me with your truth. Teach me**
**your ways.**

# A Big List of Thanks

*Let all that I am praise the LORD;*
*with my whole heart, I will praise his holy name.*
*Let all that I am praise the LORD;*
*may I never forget the good things he does for me.*
*He forgives all my sins*
*and heals all my diseases.*
*He redeems me from death*
*and crowns me with love and tender mercies.*
*He fills my life with good things.*
*My youth is renewed like the eagle's!*

PSALM 103:1-5 NLT

If you tried to make a list of all the good things in your life, it would be pretty long. A warm bed, books to read, food to eat, toys to play with, friends at school, your pets at home. You could add so much more to that list!

The person who wrote this Bible verse was thankful for everything that God had given him. He was thankful for little things, and big things, like healing, and forgiveness of sin. Remember to praise God for all these wonderful things, today.

**Father, I give you all the praise, because all good things come from you.**

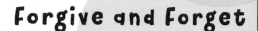

# Forgive and Forget

*I will forgive their wickedness
and will remember their sins no more.*
HEBREWS 8:12 NIV

It is so hard to forget the mean things people do to us. We tend to hold on to the hurt, but that's not what God does. He has a loving heart that forgives. When we say sorry, he makes us clean, as if we did nothing wrong. He doesn't keep a list of our mistakes. It's like they disappear.

God doesn't remember our sin, so we don't have to feel guilty or punish ourselves once we've asked for forgiveness either.

**Lord, thank you for forgiving me of the wrong things that I do. I love you.**

# A Peaceful Place

*Then Jesus said, "Let's go off by ourselves to a quiet place and rest awhile." He said this because there were so many people coming and going that Jesus and his apostles didn't even have time to eat.*

Mark 6:31 NLT

School, sports games, and playgrounds can sometimes be really crowded and noisy. Have you ever felt like you just wanted to get away from all the noise and people?

Jesus felt like this too! He knows that there are times when you just need to find a quiet space and rest from all the action. Can you find a place to be peaceful, just for a few minutes, today?

***Jesus, show me a peaceful place and meet with me there. Calm my heart and give me your quiet rest.***

# Quiet Beauty

*Your beauty should come from within you—the beauty of a gentle and quiet spirit that will never be destroyed and is very precious to God.*

1 PETER 3:4 NCV

God sees what is inside our hearts, more than what we see in the mirror. Some people are pretty on the outside but ugly on the inside. Others are gentle and quiet inside, and that is seen as beautiful in the kingdom of heaven.

The more time you spend with Jesus, the more you will reflect his character. Jesus makes you beautiful.

**Jesus, let your beauty shine through me. Let me reflect the gentle and quiet beauty that is so important to you.**

# Joy Is a Choice

> *This is the day the Lord has made.*
> *We will rejoice and be glad in it.*
> PSALM 118:24 NLT

Some days are harder than others. The sun doesn't shine or the day just feels impossible. Thankfully, God has given us joy that doesn't depend on what's going on around us.

God's joy brings us out of hiding, and shows us the beautiful things around us in the middle of a dark and stormy world. God has given this to us as a gift. Will you be joyful today?

***God, thank you that every day from you is a precious gift. Help me see your joy in everything I do today.***

# Lasting Comfort

*If the LORD had not been my help,*
*my soul would soon have lived in the land of silence.*
*When I thought, "My foot is slipping,"*
*your steadfast love, O LORD, held me up.*

PSALM 94:17-18 NRSV

Have you ever walked along a balance beam and lost your balance? It can be a little scary when you slip, and sometimes a bit embarrassing. It is quite easy to walk across, though, if someone is holding your hand to help you balance.

When God walks next to us, he gives us his hand so that we won't fall. He gives us love and support. His comfort helps us on the road ahead.

**Lord you know what I need. Help me to find your comfort and strength.**

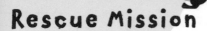

# Rescue Mission

*He will rescue the poor when they cry to him;*
*he will help the oppressed, who have*
*no one to defend them.*
*He feels pity for the weak and the needy,*
*and he will rescue them.*
*He will redeem them from oppression and violence,*
*for their lives are precious to him.*

PSALM 72:12-14 NLT

Have you seen a homeless person, begging in the streets for food or money? It can be confusing to know what to do, because they make you feel uncomfortable. Maybe you feel sorry for them, or you don't quite understand.

There are a lot of people that need help—sometimes in our own country and sometimes in other countries. Can you be a part of God's plan to help others?

*Father, help me to show your love to the people who need your help. I want to care for them like you care for them.*

128

# Peaceful Thoughts

*He will keep in perfect peace all those who trust in him, whose thoughts turn often to the Lord!*

ISAIAH 26:3 TLB

What do you think about the most in the day? Is it food, your family, friends, schoolwork, fun, chores? Wouldn't it be great if you could think about Jesus more?

When we think about so many other things, our lives feel a little messy, but the more we focus on God, the more his peace fills us. Spend some time thinking about God today.

*God, you have said you will meet all my needs and I believe you. Help me to focus my thoughts on you so that I can have peace in my heart.*

# MAY

Lord, you are forgiving and good.
You are full of love
for all who call out to you.

PSALM 86:5 NIRV

# For Us

*If God is for us, who can be against us?*
ROMANS 8:31 NIV

You can make a whirlpool by getting a lot of people together in a pool and all running around the edges going the same way. Have you ever tried that? The water becomes so strong that it is really hard to turn around and swim the other way.

God is even stronger than a whirlpool of water. When we are on his side, nothing can get in our way. He is stronger than everything.

**Heavenly Father, you are my friend. Thank you for your strong love that no one can take away.**

# In the Darkness

*The LORD is close to the brokenhearted,*
*and he saves those whose spirits have been crushed.*
PSALM 34:18 NCV

Jesus had a lot of sorrow and pain in his life. He was made fun of, hated, and hurt. He understands all our trouble.

If you are feeling sad, take some time to ask God how to help you. You are never alone. God is always close by and has never left your side.

*Father, you know my heart and my sadness. You promise to help me, because you understand. Thank you for healing me.*

# Made Right

*All need to be made right with God by his grace, which is a free gift. They need to be made free from sin through Jesus Christ. God sent him to die in our place to take away our sins.*

ROMANS 3:24-25 NCV

Sometimes life is hard to understand. But faith is simple. When we put our faith in Jesus, God sees the goodness of Jesus in our lives, not our sin. This is how God is able to forgive us.

When troubles seem overwhelming, you can run straight to God. He gave you the gift of Jesus and everything has been made right.

**God, thank you for the free gift of forgiveness through Jesus Christ. I gladly accept your gift!**

# White as Snow

*"Come, let's talk this over", says the Lord; "No matter how deep the stain of your sins, I can take it out and make you as clean as freshly fallen snow.
Even if you are stained as red as crimson,
I can make you white as wool!"*

ISAIAH 1:18 TLB

When we play outside, our clothes and shoes can get really dirty. Imagine wearing really white shoes and then stepping in mud. Yuck! That mud is like sin. God said that no sin is too bad that he can't take it away.

It's a beautiful picture. If you have told Jesus that you are sorry, you are perfectly clean. If not, don't wait another moment! Talk it over with God, and be washed clean today. All you have to do is ask.

***Thank you, God, that you forgive me and make me as clean as fresh snow!***

# Set Free!

*Live as free people, but do not use your freedom as an excuse to do evil. Live as servants of God.*
1 PETER 2:16 NCV

When prisoners are set free, everyone expects them to stop doing the bad things they were doing before. When we are set free because of Jesus, God expects us to stop doing bad things too.

The devil doesn't want us to be close to God, but we must fight back. Take a stand against the enemy with prayer and God's Word, fighting for freedom with Jesus at your side.

**Thank you, Jesus, for setting me free from sin. Help me to be strong against sin and keep serving you.**

# Better Together

*As iron sharpens iron,*
*so people can improve each other.*
PROVERBS 27:17 NCV

Friends create a lot of happiness. They bring laughter and love, and without them we'd be pretty lonely. Good friends are loyal. They love you by being truthful and sticking close by your side. God uses our friends to strengthen us.

Some of us may have a lot of friends, and others only a few, but that's okay. As long as you stand together in Jesus, you can become better together.

*Lord, thank you for the good friends that you have brought into my life. Show me which friends are good to be with, so that I can become a better friend.*

# A Beautiful Day

*I will tell about the Lord's kindness.
And I will praise him for what he has done.
He has given many good things to us.
He has been very good to the people of Israel.
The Lord has shown mercy to us.
And he has been kind to us.*

ISAIAH 63:7 ESV

God's goodness is great every day; his love is steady and always fights for us. We can show God how thankful we are by remembering how good he is and telling others about what he has done.

Even when life is hard, the list of blessings God has given you is very long. This day is beautiful because God loves you and he is so good to you.

**You are so good, God! Thank you for your kindness to me. Help me to share your love with others.**

# The Ripple Effect

*All of this is for your benefit.*
*And as God's grace reaches more and more people,*
*there will be great thanksgiving,*
*and God will receive more and more glory.*

2 CORINTHIANS 4:15 NLT

When you throw a rock into a still pond, what happens? Lots of circles of water start to show up and they get bigger and bigger as they go out. This is what God's grace is like.

When we are given grace, we feel God's love and can't wait to share it with others. Then they share our excitement and also give thanks to God. This is how we can spread the love of God all over the world. Let's give thanks to God!

**Gracious God, help me to tell about your goodness to more people. I want everyone to know how great you are!**

# God Is my Guide

*Trust in the LORD with all your heart;*
*do not depend on your own understanding.*
*Seek his will in all you do,*
*and he will show you which path to take.*
*Don't be impressed with your own wisdom.*
*Instead fear the LORD and turn away from evil.*

PROVERBS 3:5-7 NLT

When you don't know what to do, remember that God isn't trying to hide the answer from you. He wants you to go down the right path, and he will share his help when you ask.

Quiet down a little bit and listen to God. He will speak to you as you talk with him each day. You will understand his voice more and more.

*Heavenly Father, I need your help. Calm my mind and heart so I can listen to what you say and know where to go.*

# All Promises Kept

*You believe in God through Christ.*
*God raised Christ from death and gave him glory.*
*So your faith and your hope are in God.*

1 PETER 1:21 ICB

We trust God and put our hope in him because what he promises us is true. When Jesus rose again after dying on the cross, he gave us hope forever.

Jesus promised that he would rise from the dead, and he did. Now we know that every other promise he makes is true.

**Holy God, I trust that you keep all your promises and I will always have hope because of you.**

# Butterfly

*Anyone who belongs to Christ has become a new person. The old life is gone; a new life has begun!*
2 CORINTHIANS 5:17 NLT

Do you know the story of the hungry caterpillar? He eats everything he can, gets a tummy ache and then curls up into a cocoon and days later becomes a beautiful butterfly!

We can picture our life with Jesus like this. Before we knew Jesus we were like the caterpillar with a tummy ache! But now our life is as beautiful as a butterfly because Jesus is in it!

***Thank you, Lord, for giving me a new and beautiful life. I am so excited to have you with me every single day!***

# Joy Always

*Our hearts ache, but we always have joy. We are poor, but we give spiritual riches to others. We own nothing, and yet we have everything.*

2 CORINTHIANS 6:10 NLT

Happiness is an emotion that comes and goes with what's going on around us. Like sunshine on a cloudy day, happiness can be here one minute and gone the next.

But joy happens in the heart. No matter what is going on around you, God's love pours out like a fountain. You are loved so much by him, so you can always have joy.

**Loving God, I pray that your joy would overflow in me. Help those around me to know your loving salvation.**

# Love Definition

*Love is patient and kind. Love is not jealous, it does not brag, and it is not proud. Love is not rude, is not selfish, and does not become angry easily. Love does not remember wrongs done against it. Love takes no pleasure in evil, but rejoices over the truth. Love patiently accepts all things. It always trusts, always hopes, and always continues strong.*

1 CORINTHIANS 13:4-7 ICB

You are patient and kind. You are not jealous, you do not brag, you are not rude or selfish. You don't become angry easily, and you don't remember when people do wrong things to you. Does that sound like you?

Love is not just something you feel, but something you choose, even when you don't want to. It means putting other's needs before your own like Jesus did.

**Jesus, you have shown me so much love and patience. Teach me how to love like you.**

143

# Nothing Wrong

*Since we have been made right in God's sight by faith in his promises, we can have real peace with him because of what Jesus Christ our Lord has done for us.*

ROMANS 5:1 TLB

What does peace look like? Maybe it means a good night of sleep or no worries about tomorrow. Maybe it means nobody is fighting at home or your friends are all happy with you.

When we believe God's promises, we can trust in the peace of Jesus. When he is in our hearts, we are not separated from him. Nothing is wrong if we are right with God. We belong to him and he never lets us go.

**God, help me remember the peaceful promise I have through your Son, Jesus Christ.**

# One Step at a Time

*God is strong and can help you not to fall. He can bring you before his glory without any wrong in you and give you great joy. He is the only God. He is the One who saves us. To him be glory, greatness, power, and authority through Jesus Christ our Lord for all time past, now, and forever. Amen.*

JUDE 24-25 ICB

Life is like a race and sometimes we get really tired. When we feel like we can't run anymore, how do we keep going so we can finish the race?

God is powerful and majestic. He can hold you up. He carries you on his strong shoulders and keeps you from slipping. Even better, he brings you close to him. Run the race, and remember your heavenly Father. He shouts and sings songs of joy for you!

**Lift me up, mighty God, when I need help. Thank you for staying by my side.**

# Sacrifice of Praise

*Bring your petition. Come to the Lord and say, "O Lord, take away our sins; be gracious to us and receive us, and we will offer you the sacrifice of praise."*

HOSEA 14:2 TLB

Have you ever had to share your favorite toy or game with your little brother, sister, or friend that has come to stay? A sacrifice is giving up something that you really like for someone or something else.

When you have done something wrong, the Bible says to ask God to take away your sin and then to praise him for being good to you. This is your sacrifice for God: saying wonderful things about him, even when you don't feel wonderful.

**God, you deserve to hear me say great things about you. Thank you for forgiving me when I say that I am sorry.**

# God Cannot Lie

*God wanted to prove that his promise was true. He wanted them to understand clearly that his purposes never change. So God proved his promise by also making an oath. These two things cannot change. God cannot lie when he makes a promise, and he cannot lie when he makes an oath. These things encourage us who came to God for safety. They give us strength to hold on to the hope we have been given.*

HEBREWS 6:17-18 NRSV

When you break something, or hurt someone, it can be tempting to tell a lie about why you did it, or to blame it on someone else. We lie because we don't want to get in trouble. But lying actually makes you feel worse, doesn't it?

Did you know that it is not even possible for God to tell a lie? God is so good and so truthful that when he makes a promise, it has to come true.

**God, you are perfect and true. Help me to see your promises and know that you cannot lie.**

# Treasure Map

*All Scripture is inspired by God and is useful to teach us what is true and to make us realize what is wrong in our lives. It corrects us when we are wrong and teaches us to do what is right. God uses it to prepare and equip his people to do every good work.*

2 TIMOTHY 3:16-17 NLT

Have you ever had to follow a treasure map? The map will give you a picture of your surroundings, and it will tell you the direction you need to go to find the treasure.

The Bible is like a treasure map to the very best treasure of all—heaven! It tells us what life is all about and has every answer we need. It is meant to show us the right way. It will help you to know what is right and wrong and will lead you to eternal life.

**Heavenly Father, you have a great plan for my life. Thank you for the Bible. Help me to use it to follow you all my life.**

# Go Free!

*He gave himself for us so he might pay the price to free us from all evil and to make us pure people who belong only to him—people who are always wanting to do good deeds.*

TITUS 2:14 NCV

Imagine if you got put in jail for doing something wrong, and then someone else says they will take your place and let you go free. That's what Jesus did for us! We do things wrong, but Jesus said that if we believe in him, he will let us go free.

You might think this means you can keep doing wrong things and it doesn't matter. But if someone did such a kind thing for you, do you think you would keep doing bad things? No, you would want to change your behavior and do good.

*Jesus, thank you for setting me free from the wrong things that I have done. Help me to do good things because you have been so good to me.*

149

# Never Thirsty Again

*"If you only knew the gift God has for you and who you are speaking to, you would ask me, and I would give you living water …. Anyone who drinks this water will soon become thirsty again. But those who drink the water I give will never be thirsty again. It becomes a fresh, bubbling spring within them, giving them eternal life."*

JOHN 4:10, 13-15 NLT

In this verse, a woman asks Jesus for a cup of water. He tells her that he is the water she can drink and never be thirsty again. When we live with Jesus in our hearts he gives us all that we need.

Jesus loves you so much and wants you to have his gift. Will you accept it?

***Jesus, I accept you into my life. Thank you that you give me eternal life.***

# No Comparison

*Moses held his hand over the sea. All that night the
Lord drove back the sea with a strong east wind.
And so he made the sea become dry ground.
The water was split.*

Exodus 14:21 ICB

The story of Moses and the Red Sea is amazing.
God opened up the sea and people walked through
on dry land, with water on both sides. They were saved
from the enemies that were trying to capture them.

Nobody can compare to God. There is no one as
strong or mighty as he is. This same God who parted
the sea offers to give us his strength every day.

***God of all creation, you have done amazing
things. Help me to get through any trouble
with your strength.***

151

# Rich Rewards

*Do not throw away your confidence;*
*it will be richly rewarded.*
*You need to persevere so that when you have done*
*the will of God, you will receive what he has promised.*
HEBREWS 10:35-36 NIV

Hiking is a really long walk through nature. When you go for a hike, you are usually walking up and down hills or mountains. You can get tired and sore and sometimes slip a few times or have to walk through mud.

You might have heard of a word called *perseverance.* That would be what it takes to walk up a mountain. You have to work hard to get to the top, but it is beautiful when you get there. God will reward you for a life that you live for him.

***Lord, help me to keep living a life with you. I know you will reward me when I get to the top.***

# The Way to Victory

*Everyone who is a child of God conquers the world. And this is the victory that conquers the world— our faith. So the one who conquers the world is the person who believes that Jesus is the Son of God.*

1 JOHN 5:4-5 NCV

Are you bigger than the world? Not really. Is God bigger than the world? Yes! When you are on God's side, you are bigger than the world. That means that you don't have to be afraid because you believe in Jesus and he is with you.

What are you afraid of? What makes you nervous? Remember that God is bigger than all those things and he will help you.

**Thank you, Jesus, that I am bigger than the world, because I believe in you.**

# Consumed?

*I have hope*
*when I think of this:*
*The Lord's love never ends.*
*His mercies never stop.*
LAMENTATIONS 3:21-22 ICB

What is on your mind today? Are you worried about a friend? Your parents? A  test at school? Sometimes we think too much about the problem and don't think enough about the answer.

The answer is always God. When we remember that God is full of love, we can be filled with hope. We can feel much better when we think about how great God is.

***Holy Spirit, help me to think about your great love the next time I can only think about my problems, so that I can have hope.***

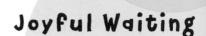

# Joyful Waiting

*I wait for the LORD, my whole being waits,*
*and in his word I put my hope.*
PSALM 130:5 NIV

Waiting for something can be very hard, and not fun at all. But sometimes waiting is exciting: waiting to tell something great, waiting for a family vacation, waiting to give someone a gift.

When we wait for good things, the waiting can be a gift too. This is how it is to wait for the Lord. We will eventually be with God forever, and waiting for that to happen is fun!

**Lord, I love waiting for you. Because I know you bring only goodness, I can wait for you with hope.**

# Inseparable

*Yes, I am sure that nothing can separate us from the love God has for us. Not death, not life, not angels, not ruling spirits, nothing now, nothing in the future, no powers, nothing above us, nothing below us, or anything else in the whole world will ever be able to separate us from the love of God that is in Christ Jesus our Lord.*

ROMANS 8:38-39 ICB

Nothing can separate you from God's love. Nothing. You don't have to be afraid, shy, or worried about anything.

You will be ok. Why? Because nothing is strong enough to take you away from the arms of your heavenly Father. This truth should be enough to make your day great!

**Father, thank you that nothing is strong enough to separate me from your love.**

# Best Treasures

*Since you became alive again, so to speak, when Christ arose from the dead, now set your sights on the rich treasures and joys of heaven where he sits beside God in the place of honor and power. Let heaven fill your thoughts; don't spend your time worrying about things down here.*

COLOSSIANS 3:1-2 TLB

Everyone around us seems to care about clothes and movies and toys. It is hard not to want to think about that all the time too.

The best treasures, though, are in heaven. That's what God wants us to think about more than things on earth. So be careful what you watch, and look at, and think about. Keep your mind on God and his Word.

**Father, please help me turn away from the things of this world, and set my heart on heaven.**

# Right Answers

*This is my prayer for you: that your love will grow more and more; that you will have knowledge and understanding with your love; that you will see the difference between good and bad and choose the good; that you will be pure and without wrong for the coming of Christ;*

PHILIPPIANS 1:9-10 ICB

When you get an answer wrong on a test, do you try to find out what the right answer is? If you can't spell a word right, do you go and ask how to spell it? It helps us get smarter when we figure out wrong and right answers.

We should love what is good, what is right, what is pure. If we ask God for the right answers, he will give it to us and we will get better and better at understanding his ways.

***Lord, help me to make wise choices with my heart every day as I live for you.***

# Stop for Thanks

*Enter his gates with thanksgiving*
*and his courts with praise;*
*give thanks to him and praise his name.*
PSALM 100:4 NIV

When you wake up in the morning it is busy. Your mom gets you up and right away you need to get dressed, get ready for school, eat breakfast, and get to class on time. It's important to do all of this, but are you forgetting something?

God wants us to remember him and thank him. It helps to be thankful toward God at the beginning of the day. Stopping to thank him gives you peace and joy that can last the whole day.

***Loving Father, thank you for giving me another day on earth. Help me be thankful. I love you.***

159

# God Sings!

*The Lord your God is with you.*
*The mighty One will save you.*
*The Lord will be happy with you.*
*You will rest in his love.*
*He will sing and be joyful about you.*

ZEPHANIAH 3:17 ICB

The Creator of the entire universe, the one who made the planets and solar systems is so much bigger than we could ever imagine. He's so big, but he cares for you. Do you ever sing when you are happy? Can you imagine what God's singing would be like?

God sings about you! That's right. He sings about you and sings around you. When it's quiet, when you're alone, when your world is crazy, he sings about his love for you.

**Father, help me hear your song today.**
**When I am nervous, alone, worried,**
**or afraid, help me to know that you**
**are happy about me.**

# The Creator

*Who has measured the oceans in the palm of his hand?*
*Who has used his hand to measure the sky?*
*Who has used a bowl to measure all the dust of the earth?*
*Who has used scales to weigh the mountains and hills?*
*God, the Holy One, says, "Can you compare me*
*to anyone? Is anyone equal to me?"*
*Look up to the skies. Who created all these stars?*
*He leads out all the army of heaven one by one.*
*He calls all the stars by name.*
*He is very strong and full of power.*
*So not one of them is missing.*

ISAIAH 40:12, 25-26 ICB

You have stopped your day to spend time with the one who created you. Maybe you have come with a list of things to talk about. Maybe you just want to hear his voice.

Today, let him tell you who he is. It will bring joy, peace, and trust into your heart.

*Holy God, I can hardly believe that you created everything. I see the stars, sun, and moon every day. Help me never to lose the excitement about your creation.*

# JUNE

The LORD God is like the sun that gives us light.
He is like a shield that keeps us safe.
The LORD blesses us with favor and honor.
He doesn't hold back anything good
from those whose lives are without blame.

PSALM 84:11 NIRV

# Wiser than You

*Did the LORD have to ask anyone
to help him understand?
Did he have to ask someone to
teach him the right way?
Who taught him what he knows?
Who showed him how to understand?*

ISAIAH 40:14 NIRV

Have you ever been blamed for something you didn't do? It doesn't seem fair. When life is unfair, it is hard to remember that God knows all things. He also knows the wrong things we have done and he forgives us for them.

Take a minute to think about how God has already fixed some of the wrong things in your life. Is there a person in your life that you can show kindness to—the way God shows kindness to you?

***Father, thank you that you are a good
judge. Even though I don't see you,
I choose to trust you.***

# Precious and Loved

*You are priceless to me.*
*I love you and honor you.*
*So I will trade other people for you.*
*I will give up other nations to save your lives.*

ISAIAH 43:4 NIRV

When you receive a card or a note from someone in your family or a friend, doesn't that make you feel good? It is nice to know that someone is thinking about you when you are not together.

God thinks about you and wants to send you encouraging notes every day. Take time to listen to what God is trying to tell you today by spending some time in prayer.

**Father, thank you for always encouraging me and showing me how much you care.**

# Care for Others

*Work hard to feed hungry people.*
*Satisfy the needs of those who are crushed.*
*Then my blessing will light up your darkness.*
*And the night of your suffering will become*
*as bright as the noonday sun.*

ISAIAH 58:10 NIRV

We throw away things that get old, dirty, or broken because we want something new. God sees things differently. He is sad that some people are poor and hungry and he reaches out to help them. One of the ways he helps those people is by asking us to care for them.

If you do everything you can for those in need, your light will shine through the darkness. As we help others, God helps us.

**Thank you, help me to know how to help those that are poor and hungry. I want to find ways to care for others.**

# A Special Place

*There are many rooms in my Father's house;*
*I would not tell you this if it were not true.*
*I am going there to prepare a place for you.*

JOHN 14:2 NCV

When you go to stay at a friend's house it is exciting. You might have a special room to stay in. They might have a nice dinner prepared for you. They let you do fun things.

God has been expecting you for a long time. Whether you realize it or not, God is preparing a place for you in heaven to be with him. Whenever you feel left out or lonely just remember how special and unique you are to God.

**Jesus, thank you that you are preparing a place for me. Thank you that my greatest joy in heaven will be spending time with you.**

# God Is Creative

*God created human beings in his image.*
*In the image of God he created them.*
*He created them male and female.*

GENESIS 1:27 ICB

Sometimes we get jealous of the movie stars and rock stars on the covers of magazines. There are days when we want to be as good looking or popular as them.

God did not create you to be just like everyone else. He created you to be special. What you are good at, someone else is not. Don't look at what other people are good at and feel bad about yourself. Instead, celebrate how wonderfully different God made you!

***God, thank you for reminding me of how special you created me to be. I am so thankful that you are a creative God.***

# A Kind Face

*Answer me, O Lord, for your steadfast love is good;*
*according to your abundant mercy, turn to me.*
PSALM 69:16 NRSV

What do you think God's face looks like when you talk to him? If you think of God as angry or mean, you probably feel a little afraid of him. If you think of him as a grumbly giant, you may not like him at all.

God is your heavenly Father. He looks like a really kind Dad. He is so happy when you come to talk to him and he wants you to trust him.

**Father, thank you that you invite me to come to you when I need you. You wait for my steps toward you and you welcome me with a big hug.**

# Stay Wonderful

*We do not give up. Our physical body is becoming
older and weaker, but our spirit inside us
is made new every day.*
2 CORINTHIANS 4:16 ICB

Have you seen a picture of your grandparents
when they were little? It's funny when you realize that
they used to be children, just like you!

As people get older, they aren't as strong or
healthy or fast as younger people. That can be a little
sad. But we aren't supposed to worry about getting
old, because one day God is going to make our
bodies wonderful again. All we need to worry about is
staying wonderful on the inside.

**Father, help me to love getting better on the
inside every day.**

169

# Delayed Obedience

*"Those who hear the teaching of God and obey it—*
*they are the ones who are truly blessed."*
LUKE 11:28 ICB

Sometimes it can be annoying listening to and obeying our parents. It can seem like they are just trying to boss us around. Your parents are really just trying to keep you safe. They don't want you to get hurt.

In the same way, God gives us directions and tells us the best way to live our lives. Sometimes it can seem like following God is like following a bunch of rules. But God has given us rules so we can live our lives safe and happy.

*Father, help me to listen to you and to be quick to obey. I want to be pleasing to you.*

# Betrayed with a Kiss

*While Jesus was still speaking, Judas came up. Judas was 1 of the 12 followers. He had many people with him. They were sent from the leading priests, the teachers of the law, and the Jewish elders. Those with Judas had swords and clubs. Judas had planned a signal for them. He had said, "The man I kiss is Jesus. Arrest him and guard him while you lead him away." So Judas went to Jesus and said, "Teacher!" and kissed him.*

MARK 14:43-45 ICB

Jesus had one of his friends hurt his feelings a lot. Judas showed the leaders who wanted to kill Jesus where he was. Judas cared more about the money they were going to give him than he did about Jesus.

We need to remember that Jesus wants our love, and he wants us to show that we care for him more than other things.

**Jesus, help me to give all my heart to you today, loving you with all that I am.**

# The Little Things

*A cheerful look brings joy to the heart;*
*good news makes for good health.*
PROVERBS 15:30 NLT

Little things are important. Offer a smile to a classmate who isn't nice to you. Say a prayer for a friend who is having a bad day. Help someone who is complaining. These little acts of helpfulness can change a person's day.

There is a reason the Holy Spirit points people out around you. Your smile might be the first smile they have gotten in a long time. Choose to give them a look of love that will bring joy to their heart.

**Father, help me to follow you even in the little things. Help my smile to brighten someone's day.**

# Good Words

*What you say can mean life or death.*
*Those who love to talk will be rewarded*
*for what they say.*
PROVERBS 18:21 ICB

Have you ever said something mean and then felt like you wanted to go back and erase what you said? The problem is that we can't take back what we say out loud. That's why we have to be careful to think before we speak.

Today, ask God to point out how you can use your words to do good. Ask him to teach you how to encourage others with your words.

***Jesus, please help me use my words for good and not evil.***

# Who are You With?

*Happy is the person who doesn't listen to the wicked.*
*He doesn't go where sinners go.*
*He doesn't do what bad people do.*
*He loves the Lord's teachings.*
*He thinks about those teachings day and night.*
PSALM 1:1-2 ICB

Think about the friends that you hang out with. How do they behave? Are they always getting in trouble, or are they people you can trust?

When you surround yourself with people who know and love God, you can help each other do the right things. Good friends will not get you in trouble because they will help you make good decisions.

***God, give me good friends who know you so I can keep following you even when it is difficult.***

174

# Hiding His Word

*I have stored up your word in my heart,*
*that I might not sin against you.*
PSALM 119:11 ESV

Do you find it hard or easy to learn memory verses? Are there some you can think of right now that you have learned at church?

One of the best ways to keep God's Word in your heart is to memorize parts of the Bible. When you memorize something, you repeat it in your head. This simple action makes you think about the Word of God, and will help you remember it when you need it the most.

**Father, please give me the memory to keep your words in my heart so they will be there when I need them the most.**

# Real Life

*Keep me from looking at worthless things.*
*Let me live by your word.*
PSALM 119:37 ICB

There are a lot of things in this world that we can spend hours thinking about. Everybody has something. It can be sports, movies, books, fashion, or something else. What do you think about?

God gave us things in life to enjoy, but we need to remember that some things take up so much time that we forget to think about God or spend time with him. We might forget to think about people that need our help or our love. Loving God means finding life in the right things.

**Dear God, help me to know when things are getting in the way of loving you and loving others.**

# Meditation

*Help me understand how your rules direct me to live.
Then I may think deeply about the wonderful things
you have done.*

PSALM 119:27 NIRV

Spending time with God is never wasted. Sometimes it may seem boring. Maybe whenever you try to spend time in prayer you get tired and fall asleep, or you just can't concentrate.

No matter what happens when you pray, God will teach you something. Take time to think about all the great things God has done. Your list will never end. The more time you spend with him, the more you will know his voice.

**Father, I don't want my faith to be boring. Help me to hear your words so I can live a wonderful life with you.**

# Open My Eyes

*Open my eyes to see the wonderful things in your teachings.*
PSALM 119:18 ICB

Do you sometimes think you have heard all the same stories in the Bible? Do you realize that even older people who have read the Bible for fifty years are still finding things that they didn't see before?

God's Word always has something to tell us. If you feel yourself wanting to doze off the next time you read your Bible, ask God to show you something new. All you need to do is ask.

**Holy Spirit, I ask that you open my eyes and show me something new and awesome in the Bible, today.**

# My Counselors

*Your rules give me pleasure.*
*They give me good advice.*
PSALM 119:24 ICB

Parents, grandparents, other family members, and friends can help us in hard times. We don't need to try and figure out God's way on our own. God gave us people who can share their stories with us so that we know we are not alone.

Are there things you want to share with other people you trust? Ask God to make you brave enough to ask the right people for help.

**Father, thank you for the people that are in my life that will be able to help me when I cannot do everything by myself.**

# He Remembers

*Though a thousand generations pass he never forgets his promise, his covenant with Abraham and Isaac.*
PSALM 105:8-9 TLB

God made a promise with Abraham that his children would be as many as the stars in the sky. There are still people in the world that have come from Abraham. A lot of people. God didn't forget his promise.

Aren't you glad we have a God we can count on?

*Dear God, thank you for keeping your promise to Abraham and for sending Jesus so I could know you. I am so glad I can count on you.*

# To the Rescue

*I am happy when I have weaknesses, insults, hard times, sufferings, and all kinds of troubles. All these things are for Christ. And I am happy, because when I am weak, then I am truly strong.*

2 CORINTHIANS 12:10 ICB

Sometimes we see the best in people when things go wrong. If someone gets hurt, we see others come to help. If someone is being bullied, we see others stand up for that person.

When things happen that aren't very good, remember that Jesus will come to your rescue. He will send others to help you, and he will remind you of his love and peace. Then you will know that God is good.

*Father, help me to turn to you when things are hard. I want to see your strength that helps me get through everything.*

# It Is Finished

*After Jesus drank he said, "It is finished." Then he bowed his head and died.*

JOHN 19:30 NIRV

When Jesus died on the cross it would have been a sad day. But when Jesus said, "It is finished," he didn't mean that it was the end. He meant it in the same way you would finish coloring a picture and say, "It is finished."

Jesus completed God's plan for rescuing us. He did this by dying on the cross and then coming alive again a few days later. Jesus finished the job and now we get to have eternal life.

**Thank you, Lord, that your finished work on the cross has given me eternal life.**

# Fueled by Love

*I know what you are doing. You work long and hard. I know you can't put up with evil people. You have tested those who claim to be apostles but are not. You have found out that they are liars. You have been faithful and have put up with a lot of trouble because of me. You have not given up.*

REVELATION 2:2-3 NIRV

Do you remember finally getting the toy that you had been wanting for so long? It is such a good feeling to get something you really wanted. Do you still feel that way about that toy? Sometimes our joy for something goes away over time.

Jesus felt like this could happen with people that believe in him. We might be really happy to have Jesus in our hearts, but we could also forget about this happiness if we forget to thank him and spend time with him.

*Jesus, I know that you want my love. Help me to always be grateful for having you in my life.*

183

# Fear Not

*There is no fear in love. Instead, perfect love drives away fear. That's because fear has to do with being punished. The one who fears does not have perfect love.*

1 JOHN 4:18 NIRV

Everyone has something they are afraid of. It might be the imaginary monster under the bed, or a fear of not making any friends. Your parents can be afraid sometimes too.

It doesn't matter who you are, Jesus' love is still stronger than fear. Don't be afraid because his love is perfect. His love does not punish you, or hurt you, or make you feel afraid. His love gives you peace.

**Jesus, thank you that your love is bigger than anything I am afraid of.**

184

# The Story Isn't Finished

*When I saw him, I fell down at his feet like a dead man. He put his right hand on me and said, "Do not be afraid! I am the First and the Last. I am the One who lives. I was dead, but look: I am alive forever and ever! And I hold the keys of death and where the dead are."*
REVELATION 1:17-18 ICB

Do you know what the first and last letter of the alphabet are? Does any letter come before A? Does any letter come after Z?

There is no one before God and no one after God. He is everything from the beginning to the end. So, you don't have to worry about anything else because he is in control of everything A to Z!

*Jesus, thank you that you were there from the beginning and that you will be there at the end. I want to be a part of your plan from A to Z.*

# Together

There is neither Jew nor Gentile,
neither slave nor free, nor is there male and female,
for you are all one in Christ Jesus.
GALATIANS 3:28 NIV

Do you ever have to divide into groups of boys or girls? Maybe you have to divide a group into ages? There are often choices about which side we are going to be on, but the Bible says that we are all part of God's big family.

Make sure you include everyone in the family of God. He doesn't want people to be separated; he wants us all to be together!

*Jesus, help me to see everyone as part of one big family, all trying to get along so we can please you.*

# Quick Fix

*Let's not get tired of doing what is good. At just the right time we will reap a harvest of blessing if we don't give up.*

GALATIANS 6:9 NLT

When you plant a seed in a pot and wait for it to grow, it can take a very long time for a little sprout to show. Wouldn't it take even longer to see flowers on the plant?

God says that sometimes the results of our good works can take time to start showing, just like that seed being planted in a pot. We need to have patience and keep doing good. At the right time, God will show us the good that has come from doing the right thing.

*Father, I want to follow you and be a good example. Help me to be patient while I wait for the results of my good works to show.*

# Time to Rest

*Let my soul be at rest again,*
*for the LORD has been good to me.*

PSALM 116:7 NLT

There are so many things to do in a day! Go to school, hang out with friends, go to practice, talk to family. Being excited for things is good, but we also want to take time to rest.

There is a reason that we have to sleep each night. It may get annoying when your parents tell you to go to bed, but without sleep, we cannot do any of the fun things we want to do. God calls us to rest in a different way. He wants us to rest our hearts. He wants us to sit down for a few minutes and think about him. Take a little time to rest with God today.

**Jesus, help me to slow down and see how important it is to rest.**

# You Can't Control the Rain

*He covers the heavens with clouds,*
*prepares rain for the earth,*
*makes grass grow on the hills.*
*The LORD takes pleasure in those who fear him,*
*in those who hope in his steadfast love.*

PSALM 147:8, 11 NRSV

How is the weather where you are? Has it been raining? Have you had a lot of sun? Is it too hot, or too cold, or is it just right?

You can't control the weather, and you can't always control things happening to you. But you can control what to do when the weather is bad or when life is hard. Ask God to give you hope and peace. He will always do that.

*God, thank you that you control what happens in my life. Help me to be thankful that you care enough to help me grow.*

# Be Your Best

*He knows how we were made.*
*He remembers that we are dust.*
PSALM 103:14 ICB

Can you jump higher than a building? Can you walk through walls? Can you walk on water? Of course not! Our bodies weren't made to do things like that.

God made our bodies and he didn't make a mistake. We were made to live a great life, but he didn't want us all to be superheroes. God wanted us to be the best we can be, and that is enough!

*Father, you designed me exactly how you wanted me to be. Help me to love the body that you have given me and keep it healthy.*

# Work Hard

*People who refuse to work want things
and get nothing.
But the desires of people who work hard
are completely satisfied.*

PROVERBS 13:4 NIRV

Working hard can actually feel really good. When you get a job done, you feel like you have done well.

Sometimes when we are asked to do a job around the house, we complain. We might take a long time to do the job. We might wish we were doing something else. The Bible says that we will be rewarded if we have a good attitude about doing work. Can you change your heart about doing jobs others have asked you to do?

**Father, help me to do the jobs that I am asked to do with joy and thankfulness.**

# Don't Quit

*We can rejoice, too, when we run into problems and trials, for we know that they are good for us—they help us learn to be patient. And patience develops strength of character in us and helps us trust God more each time we use it until finally our hope and faith are strong and steady.*

ROMANS 5:3-4 TLB

When you are running a relay race, you have to pass a baton—a thick stick—to the next person before they can start running their part of the race. If you are waiting for the baton, you cheer your team on, telling the runner to keep going and not to give up.

The Bible says that we shouldn't give up on doing good. When we always try to do the right thing, we will become better and quicker at doing right. Don't quit; keep going!

*Father, I don't want to give up. Help me to keep going for you.*

# JULY

Praise the LORD, because he is good;
sing praises to him, because it is pleasant.

PSALM 135:3 NCV

# Enjoy Today

*Hear, O Israel: The LORD is our God, the LORD alone.
You shall love the LORD your God with all your heart,
and with all your soul, and with all your might.*

DEUTERONOMY 6:4-5 NRSV

Are you always thinking about the next big event?
Whose birthday party is next week? When do you get
to visit family? When is your friend coming over?

God asks you to focus on him with all your heart,
all your soul, and all your might. He doesn't want you
to miss what is happening right now! Enjoy the day he
has made for you.

**Father, help me love you with all that I am, today
and forever.**

# Cheer!

*Let us not give up meeting together. Some are in the habit of doing this. Instead, let us encourage one another with words of hope. Let us do this even more as you see Christ's return approaching.*
HEBREWS 10:25 NIRV

What does the team mascot look like at your school? Do you have one, or know what it is? A mascot is someone dressed up like a character, and they are there to cheer on the sports team to help them win!

Good friends take the time to cheer each other on. They show up when their friends need them, and they say kind, thoughtful things. Be thankful for those friends in your life, and make sure you are a good friend too!

**God, please remind me be positive and cheerful toward my friends.**

# Peaceful Thoughts

*God's peace will keep your hearts and minds in Christ Jesus. The peace that God gives is so great that we cannot understand it.*

PHILIPPIANS 4:7 ICB

Did you know that what you do comes from what you think about? If you start to think about your favorite food you will probably start looking for something to eat.

It's the same way with our feelings. If we think about how much we don't like someone, we are more likely to be mean to them. When we have a good feeling about someone, we are kind to them. God wants us to think good things, and that will give us great peace.

*Holy Spirit, please teach me how to control my thoughts. Help me to choose to think about good things so that I have peace in my life.*

# Free

*Jesus said to the Jews who believed in him,*
*"If you continue to obey my teaching,*
*you are truly my followers. Then you will know the*
*truth. And the truth will make you free."*
JOHN 8:31-32 ICB

Do you know the game called "Stuck in the Mud" or "Freeze Tag"? When you get tagged, you have to freeze, and you can't move until another player sets you free by going through your legs!

Jesus said that his truth sets you free. It's kind of like we are stuck in sin and then the truth of Jesus' forgiveness sets us free. That's pretty good news, right?

**Lord, fill my mind with the truth of your forgiveness that will set me free.**

# Eternal Life

*These children are people with physical bodies. So Jesus himself became like them and had the same experiences they have. He did this so that, by dying, he could destroy the one who has the power of death. That one is the devil. Jesus became like men and died so that he could free them. They were like slaves all their lives because of their fear of death.*

HEBREWS 2:14-15 ICB

Have you ever been losing a game and then someone says that they would like to start the game again? It's like you've been given a second chance to win!

Jesus died on the cross, but then he rose again, which means he came back to life! Jesus did this to show us that even though we will die one day, we will also live again, just like he did. Don't be afraid, you have been given eternal life!

**Jesus, thank you that you beat death and gave me eternal life.**

# Powerful Love

*We know how much God loves us, and we have put our trust in his love. God is love, and all who live in love live in God, and God lives in them.*

1 John 4:16 NLT

God's love for you is the most powerful force in the entire universe. Nothing has the power to stop it.

We get to be a part of this love. The Bible says that if we live in God's love, that his love will be in us and we can share it with others. Think about God's incredible love for you today.

*Father, thank you that your love for me is stronger than anything else in life. Help me to share your love with others.*

# Endless Love

*The Lord shows mercy and is kind.*
*He does not become angry quickly,*
*and he has great love.*

PSALM 103:8 ICB

You know when you have done something wrong and you think your parents are going to yell at you? You expected them to be angry, but instead they treated you kindly.

God has that kind of love for you. He is full of mercy and grace, which means that he is kind to you even when you have done something wrong. He doesn't get angry quickly and he makes sure that you know of his great love.

**Father, thank you for your love. Help me do the right thing even though I know you will show me kindness no matter what.**

# Rules, Rules, Rules

*In the kingdom of God, eating and drinking are not important. The important things are living right with God, peace, and joy in the Holy Spirit.*

ROMANS 14:17 ICB

Do you have rules at school, or at home? You probably aren't allowed to jump on the couches, eat candy in the morning, or talk after you have gone to bed. Rules can be annoying, but there is something greater about them. They keep you safe and healthy.

Jesus did not come to give us a bunch of rules. He doesn't want you to just obey him. He knows that his ways will help you to know his life, joy, and peace as you become his friend.

*Father, thank you that your kingdom is about so much more than rules. Please help me know your love that gives me the strength to obey you, so I will walk in righteousness, peace, and joy.*

# Because of Love

*That Christ may dwell in your hearts through faith,*
*as you are being rooted and grounded in love.*

EPHESIANS 3:17 NRSV

As a plant grows, we usually only see what is happening above the dirt. We admire the leaves and the colors of the flowers. But no plant looks like that without some strong, sturdy roots in the soil. Those roots keep the plant growing healthy and beautiful.

We become beautiful people when we let God be like our roots. If you can remind yourself every day that God loves you, you will show his love on the outside and that will make you even more beautiful.

*Father, give me the grace to trust your love for me. Help me grow my roots in your love and nothing else.*

# Much Better

*Let me hear of your unfailing love each morning,*
*for I am trusting you.*
*Show me where to walk,*
*for I give myself to you.*
PSALM 143:8 NLT

Imagine yourself walking down a hallway when suddenly the lights go out. Only a moment ago you knew where you were going, but now you aren't so sure. You try to remember where the door was and how far away you were from the wall.

Sometimes we can get confused and find ourselves in difficult situations. God has given us the Bible as a guide to help us through each day. He has also given us the Holy Spirit who lives inside of us and can teach us the right way.

**Father, thank you that you are who you say you are. Help me to believe in you even when I am confused.**

# Wisdom with Age

*In the same way, younger men should be willing to be under older men. And all of you should be very humble with each other.*
*"God is against the proud,*
*but he gives grace to the humble."*
1 PETER 5:5 ICB

Who is older than you? You parents, your teachers, your babysitter. When you are young, most people are older than you. Now think about how much older they are. Is it 10 years? 20 years? 30 years, or even more?

Older people know more because they have lived a lot longer than you have. Make sure, if you trust these people, that you listen to what they say and understand that they know better than you do. This is what respect is all about.

*Father, thank you for the older people in my life who care about me. Help me to always respect them.*

# Get a Glimpse

*A single day in your courtyards is better
than a thousand anywhere else.
I would rather guard the door of the house of my God
than live in the tents of sinful people.*

PSALM 84:10 NIRV

Imagine you are standing in the middle of two camps. On one side is a whole lot of little tents, only big enough to fit one or two people. On the other side is a beautiful huge castle, big enough to fit thousands. Where would you rather be? In the tents or at the door of the castle?

The writer of this verse said they would rather be at the door of God's great house than to be anywhere else. Don't you agree?

*Father, thank you that you are preparing a place for me to be with you forever. Help me to remember that being with you is more important than anything else in life.*

# Thoughts on Beauty

*Your beauty should not come from outward
adornment, such as elaborate hairstyles and the
wearing of gold jewelry or fine clothes.
Rather, it should be that of your inner self,
the unfading beauty of a gentle and quiet spirit,
which is of great worth in God's sight.*
1 PETER 3:3-4 NIV

When was the last time you had a haircut? Did your
parents cut it, or did they take you to a hairdresser?
Have you ever had a haircut that you really didn't like?
Sometimes we care a lot about what we look like on
the outside.

God isn't bothered by what your hair looks like,
is he? He loves your whole person, inside and out,
and what he thinks is the most attractive is to have a
gentle and quiet heart. Isn't it great to know that God
cares about the right stuff?

*Lord, help me to see myself the way
you do. Help me to know what you
have placed within me.*

# A Happy Yes

*Restore to me the joy of your salvation,*
*and make me willing to obey you.*
PSALM 51:12 NLT

Do you remember a time when you didn't want to do what your parents asked you to do? Maybe they told you to go upstairs and brush your teeth and you chose to ignore them because you didn't want to go to bed. We have a lot of choices to obey every single day.

You probably know that in the end it feels really good to do the right thing. When you obey, it makes your parents happy too! God would love us to be joyful about obeying him as well.

*Lord, your way is best. Help me to always obey you and to be joyful about obeying others.*

# Kindness

*Be kind and compassionate to one another, forgiving each other, just as in Christ God forgave you.*
EPHESIANS 4:32 NIV

It can be fun to look for creative ways to be kind. You might decide to pick a flower for your mother, or do the dishes without being asked. You might make a card for your friend, or get a Band-Aid for your little brother who hurt his knee.

The more you look for ways to be kind, the more kindness will become a part of who you are. The same thing happens with forgiveness. Every time we choose to forgive other people, it becomes easier to be a person who forgives!

*Lord, help me to always follow your example of kindness and love. Help me to be quick to forgive just as you forgave me.*

# You are Rich!

*Tell them to use their money to do good.
They should be rich in good works and generous
to those in need, always being ready to share with
others. By doing this they will be storing up their
treasure as a good foundation for the future so that
they may experience true life.*
1 TIMOTHY 6:18-19 NLT

It's hard to save up money. You are too young to work, so you need your parents to pay for things until you get a few dollars. But money is not the only way you can be rich.

If you don't have a lot of money, but you have a lot of extra time, you can use your time to bless others. What do you do during your free time? What ways could you be showing God's love to other people?

**Father, thank you for giving me a lot of love. Help me to share your love with those in need.**

# No Surprises

*Dear friends, don't be surprised by the terrible things happening to you. The trouble you are having has come to test you. So don't feel as if something strange were happening to you.*

1 PETER 4:12 NIRV

Strange things happen sometimes. Would you think it was strange if you found an elephant in your backyard? What about if your mother served you broccoli for breakfast? That would be strange!

When we go through hard times, the Bible says that we shouldn't think it is strange. God knew that life would be tough sometimes. He said to expect those hard times so you can remember that God is in control and will take care of you. Now that's not strange; it's wonderful!

***God, help me to get through the tough times because I know and I believe that you are good.***

# Help Me Get Dressed

*God has chosen you and made you his holy people. He loves you. So you should always clothe yourselves with mercy, kindness, humility, gentleness, and patience.*
COLOSSIANS 3:12 NCV

Every day when you step out of bed, you have a choice to make. Am I going to be happy or sad? Nice or mean? Positive or negative?

God tells us to pick out our attitude like we pick out our clothes. We do not have to always pretend like we are the happiest person in the world, but even on bad days we have a choice. You could be the person that brightens someone's day by giving them a little taste of the joy you have found in Jesus.

**Father God, today I ask that you help me choose to have a better mood and make good choices for you.**

# Ready to Forgive

*Be gentle and ready to forgive; never hold grudges.
Remember, the Lord forgave you,
so you must forgive others.*
COLOSSIANS 3:13 TLB

Have you ever had a fight with a friend that lasted for days? It can be pretty sad to be mad at someone for a long time. It doesn't feel great. That's what a grudge is, staying mad, instead of letting go and forgiving.

How do you forgive people? You just do! The Bible doesn't say that there are words that we need to use, or that we have to feel good about someone. It just says to forgive. It starts with saying in your heart, or out loud, that you forgive that person. The cool thing is that Jesus does the rest for you; you just have to let go.

***Lord, you have forgiven me. Please give me the grace to forgive those who have done wrongs things to me.***

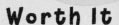

# Worth It

*Be joyful that you are taking part in Christ's sufferings.
Then you will have even more joy when
Christ returns in glory.*
1 Peter 4:13 NIRV

Running a race can be fun, but if it is a long race
it can be really hard. You start to get tired, your legs
start to hurt, and you begin to feel thirsty. But if you
push through, you will finish the race, and you might
even win!

Our life with God can be like a race. It can be hard
at times. You might not feel joyful, and sad things
might have happened to you. If you keep living with
God's love in your heart and remember to love him
too, then you can remember to smile.

***Jesus, give me joy on those days when I find it
hard. Help me to remember that I have
heaven waiting for me.***

213

# Sparrows Don't Worry

*"Look at the birds of the air; they neither sow nor reap nor gather into barns, and yet your heavenly Father feeds them. Are you not of more value than they? And can any of you by worrying add a single hour to your span of life?"*

MATTHEW 6:26-27 NRSV

Do you know how sparrows get their food? How do they find safe places to rest at night? God designed nature so creatures like birds don't have to worry. Sparrows find big beautiful trees to keep safe in at night, and they wake up to find their breakfast in the dirt in the morning.

God doesn't want us to worry either. He says that he cares even more for us than the sparrows. If those little birds don't have to worry about life, then neither do you! Trust God to take care of you.

**God, thank you for your amazing creation. Help me to always trust that you will take care of me.**

# others First

*You are still following the ways of the world. Some of you are jealous. Some of you argue. So aren't you following the ways of the world? Aren't you acting like ordinary human beings?*

1 CORINTHIANS 3:3 NIRV

Have you ever wanted the toy that your friend just got for their birthday? Have you ever been jealous of your brother and sister because they got special time with your mom or dad?

When we get grumpy about what others have, we are not thinking about their best. We fight because we are only thinking about ourselves. God wants us to be different. He wants us to think about others first, so that we are happy when something good happens to them. Can you change your attitude toward other people today?

**God, move my heart to care for others rather than to only care about what I want. Help me to be happy for others.**

# Our Creator

*When I look at the night sky and*
*see the work of your fingers—*
*the moon and the stars you set in place—*
*what are mere mortals that you should think about them,*
*human beings that you should care for them?*
*Yet you made them only a little lower than God*
*and crowned them with glory and honor.*
PSALM 8:3-5 NLT

In the creation story, God created light and dark, water and sky, land and plants, the sun, moon, and stars, fish and birds, and animals. He called them all "good." Then, he went on and created humans and called them, "very good." When God was creating, he got really excited about each new creation, but he got especially excited when he created humans.

Remember that you are a special creation. He gets excited when he thinks about you. You will always be special to him.

**Oh God, it is amazing that you, the God who created the universe, care about me. Help me to remember this every day.**

# Praise the Lord!

*Let all that I am praise the LORD.*
*I will praise the LORD as long as I live.*
*I will sing praises to my God with my dying breath.*
PSALM 146:1-2 NLT

When you do something really well, like get all your spelling right, or have a great swimming lesson, or clean up your bedroom, you will probably hear your parents or teacher tell you that you have done a good job. It feels good to know that someone is happy about what you have done.

The word *praise* means to tell someone how good they are at something. When the Bible says to praise the Lord, it means that we understand that God is a really good God and we thank him for that. So tell him, every day, in every way!

**Lord, you are so good to me and to others. Thank you so much for being such a great God.**

# Tug-of-War

*"You must give your whole heart to him.
You must hold out your hands to him for help.
Put away the sin that is in your hand.
Let no evil live in your tent.
Then you can lift up your face without shame.
You can stand strong without fear."*

JOB 11:13-15 ICB

Do you know the game tug-of-war? You and your team hold on to one end of a really big rope, and another team hold tight to the other end. You pull in different directions and try to pull the other team over the line.

At times, it feels like we are in a tug-of-war of good and bad. We want to do the right thing, and then we are pulled toward doing the wrong thing. God says that if you keep thinking about him and what he would want, it will be easier for the good side to win!

*Lord, thank you that your way is the best. Help me to become stronger and stronger with you.*

# Rescued

*I will shout for joy and sing your praises,
for you have ransomed me.*
PSALM 71:23 NLT

A boy carved a little boat out of a scrap of wood. He decided to test it out in a stream but the stream carried away his boat faster than he could follow it. A few weeks later, as he and his dad were in town, they saw his boat in a shop window. He would have to pay to get his boat back, and he did because it was so special to him.

This is kind of what Jesus did for us. He is like the boy and we are like the boat that he made. Jesus gave up his life to get you back. He loves you that much!

***Oh, Lord, you created me, but I was lost until you found me. Thank you for buying me back!***

# Ask Him

*Don't worry about anything; instead, pray about everything. Tell God what you need, and thank him for all he has done. Then you will experience God's peace, which exceeds anything we can understand. His peace will guard your hearts and minds as you live in Christ Jesus.*

PHILIPPIANS 4:6-7 NLT

The great thing about God is that he always knows what you need. When you need someone to talk to, he's there. When you need help, he's there. He is never going to leave you.

It is easy to forget that we can pray to God even when we don't feel like he needs to give us anything. God wants to hear about both the good and the bad. Talk to him and let him give your heart peace because you know that he cares.

**Lord, I give you my worries and thank you for your promises.**

# Signs

*"Stand where the roads cross and look.*
*Ask where the old way is.*
*Ask where the good way is, and walk on it.*
*If you do, you will find rest for yourselves.*
*But you have said, 'We will not walk on the good way!'"*

JEREMIAH 6:16 ICB

If you go for a drive, or even out for a walk, you will see a lot of signs. Signs point you to the way that you want to go, and they tell you about the place you just passed. If you see a food sign, you know there is food inside. If you see a sign that says, "Do not enter," you know that you can't go there.

When you have decisions to make, like whether to practice your instrument or play a game, think about the kinds of signs that God gives you. Would he say, "This is good," or, "This is bad." Learn God's ways because they are always right.

**God, help me to understand and listen to you when I have to make important decisions.**

221

# The Do-Over

*The faithful love of the LORD never ends!*
*His mercies never cease.*
*Great is his faithfulness;*
*his mercies begin afresh each morning.*
LAMENTATIONS 3:22-23 NLT

Have you ever seen a movie where the person gets to go back in time and do the whole day again? Maybe the person is able to fix a mistake and make everything go the right way.

Living in God's grace is kind of like getting to start over each day. God does not hold anything from yesterday against you. He has new blessings for you each morning.

*Jesus, I receive your love and forgiveness this morning. Help me to focus on today and not worry about yesterday.*

# Two Are Better

*Two people are better off than one, for they can help
each other succeed. If one person falls, the other can
reach out and help. But someone who falls alone
is in real trouble. Likewise, two people lying close
together can keep each other warm.
But how can one be warm alone?*

ECCLESIASTES 4:9-11 NLT

Have you ever been so cold that you have snuck
into your parents' room to snuggle up in their warm
bed? If no one was in that bed, it wouldn't be warm,
would it?

God thinks that people need each other, that's
why he made so many of us, and that's why he gives
us family and friends. When you find people that you
trust, remember to be kind and helpful to them, and
make sure you ask them for help when you need it.
God created us to love each other.

***Jesus, thank you for family and friends
that I can be truthful with. Help me to love
others by being helpful.***

# The Greatest Commandment

> "'Love the Lord your God with all your heart and with all your soul and with all your mind.' This is the first and greatest commandment."
>
> MATTHEW 22:37 NIV

It's kind of interesting to think of love as a rule, isn't it? Your parents will tell you to sit still, or eat your dinner, or go to bed, but they don't usually command you to love them.

Well, God says that loving is the most important command of all. Do you know why? Because every other rule can be followed if you are someone that loves God and loves others.

*Jesus, thank you for loving me so much. Help me to show my love for you in everything I do today.*

# AUGUST

O give thanks to the LORD,
for he is good,
for his steadfast love endures forever.

PSALM 136:1 NRSV

# God's Promises

*Don't be afraid, for I am with you.*
*Don't be discouraged, for I am your God.*
*I will strengthen you and help you.*
*I will hold you up with my victorious right hand.*

ISAIAH 41:10 NLT

It is fun to receive trophies and awards for things like dance competitions, art shows, and sports tournaments. It can also be sad when you don't get the award. When we only think about the trophies, we might forget that enjoying the activity is better than an award.

God doesn't have winners or losers. When you love God, you are already a winner along with everyone else who loves God. Don't be afraid or sad; you are a champion for God!

*God, it is so nice to know that even when I mess up, you are there. Thank you that every day that I love you is a day that I am winning.*

# Dark to Light

*He has rescued us from the kingdom of darkness and transferred us into the Kingdom of his dear Son, who purchased our freedom and forgave our sins.*
COLOSSIANS 1:13-14 NLT

If you've ever moved to a different house, you probably felt a lot of different emotions. You might be sad, excited, and scared all in one day, or one hour!

The Bible talks about us moving from darkness to light. That means that once we might have been stuck in the wrong place, but God has shown us a new way to live. Living in God's light is the best place to be.

**Lord, thank you for moving me from a dark place, to a wonderful light place. Help me to remember the you have the best kingdom.**

# A Broken Heart

*The Lord is close to the brokenhearted.*
*He saves those whose spirits have been crushed.*
PSALM 34:18 ICB

Jesus knows what it's like to have a broken heart. He was hurt by people he cared about and it was hard for him to die on the cross. That's why the Bible says he can be near to us when we are having a hard time because he understands.

Are you having a hard time, today? Do you know someone who is sad, or mad, or upset? Remember that Jesus cares and he will rescue you when you need it the most.

***God, I am so grateful that you understand when I have a bad day. Thank you that you are always near me.***

# Faith without Seeing

*It was by faith that Abraham obeyed when God called him to leave home and go to another land that God would give him as his inheritance. He went without knowing where he was going.*

HEBREWS 11:8 NLT

Imagine if someone gave you a picture of a place in the world and then said, "You need to go there." You would want to know where it was, how to get there, and what you would need to bring. In the Bible, God asked Abraham to go somewhere, and Abraham didn't even know where. He just went!

True faith always obeys God. In fact, our obedience to God is what shows us that our faith is real. Abraham took one step at a time before the next one was shown to him. Will you let God show you what your next step is?

**Father God, help me to trust you more and lead me each step of the way.**

# Blind Trust

*You love him even though you have never seen him;*
*though not seeing him, you trust him; and even now*
*you are happy with the inexpressible joy that comes*
*from heaven itself. And your further reward for trusting*
*him will be the salvation of your souls.*

1 Peter 1:8-9 TLB

It can be difficult to believe in God because we cannot see him. We like having our friends and family close because they can give us hugs and we can see their face when we talk to them.

When God created Adam and Eve, they could walk with him in the Garden of Eden. Now, because of sin, we can no longer look at God's face directly but he still walks with us. God is close to us even when we don't know that he is. This is why we can love him and trust him even though we cannot see him.

*Lord, I know you are real even though I cannot see you with my eyes. Thank you for being with me.*

# Strength

*I can do all things through him who strengthens me.*
PHILIPPIANS 4:11-13 NLT

What does the Bible mean when it says we can do all things? Can we fly like a bird? Can we make a lollipop appear? Can we ride a tiger? God doesn't mean he is a magician, God means that we can do what he created us to do if we just ask him.

When we have a bad day, get in an argument with a friend, or even lose someone we love, God can give us the strength to keep going. You will find that God will bless you so you can do more than you ever thought you could do.

**God, thank you for your strength. I can do everything because I have you.**

231

# Deer Feet

*The LORD and King gives me strength.*
*He makes my feet like the feet of a deer.*
*He helps me walk on the highest places.*

HABAKKUK 3:19 NIRV

When God created deer, he gave them feet that would allow them to do everything they needed to do. They were made to gallop across a field at top speed, jump the highest fence, and scramble quickly up a steep hill. Our power does not come from our legs like a deer, but from prayer.

God is your strength today. He will give you what it takes to walk with him through the valleys and mountains. He will help you stand even if you fall.

**Thanks, God, for giving me strength and confidence and for helping me stand back up when I fall.**

# Fix Your Thoughts

*Fix your thoughts on what is true, and honorable, and right, and pure, and lovely, and admirable. Think about things that are excellent and worthy of praise.*

PHILIPPIANS 4:8 NLT

Have you ever tried to hammer a nail into a piece of wood? It might be hard, but once that nail is hammered in, it's very tough to get it out of the wood again.

The Bible says to fix our thoughts of good things. That is kind of like sticking our thoughts strongly into right, lovely, and pure things. If we do this enough times, they will be stuck in our minds, just like that nail hammered into the wood. Choose today to believe you are loved and cared for and that God will never leave you.

*Lord, I choose today to fix my thoughts on you and all your good things.*

# Forgetting

*I focus on this one thing: Forgetting the past and looking forward to what lies ahead, I press on to reach the end of the race and receive the heavenly prize for which God, through Christ Jesus, is calling us.*

PHILIPPIANS 3:13-14 NLT

Have you ever got to school and realized that you had forgotten your books, or your sports shirt, or your water bottle? Forgetting things can be really annoying.

There is a good kind of forgetting. The Bible says to forget your mistakes from yesterday, last week, or last year. Instead you should look forward to a wonderful life in Jesus.

**Lord, thank you for forgiving me of wrong things that I did yesterday. I choose today to forgive myself and to look forward to everything that you have planned for me.**

# Forgiveness

*"If you do not forgive the sins of other people,
your Father will not forgive your sins."*
MATTHEW 6:15 NIRV

Sometimes, other people can be just plain mean!
They can say rude things, cheat, or even steal from us.
It hurts when that happens.

Nobody is perfect. Sometimes we are the mean
people who are unkind to others. Hopefully, when this
happens, we ask for forgiveness from the person we
hurt and from God. If we ask for true forgiveness,
God will forgive and forget everything.

***Jesus, please forgive me and help me to
forgive people who have done wrong to me.***

# Temptation

*He himself suffered when he was tempted.*
*Now he is able to help others who are being tempted.*
HEBREWS 2:18 NIRV

Jesus knows what it's like to want to take the easy way out. When he knew his death was near, he prayed for another way. In the end, he made the choice to do what was the best for others.

We are supposed to be like Jesus. Sometimes it is difficult to make the right decision. It seems like it would be so much easier to take the easy path. We can find strength in Jesus because he knows how we feel and he will help us do the right thing.

**Father, help me to stand strong when I am tempted to do the wrong thing. I want to always follow you and do the right thing.**

# Chosen by God

*You have been chosen by God himself—you are priests of the King, you are holy and pure, you are God's very own—all this so that you may show to others how God called you out of the darkness into his wonderful light.*

1 PETER 2:9 TLB

We believe what people tell us about who we are. If we are smart at school, people might say we have good brains. If we are good at sports, we might become popular. If we look good, people might say that they like us.

God doesn't think those things are the most important. He calls us loved and amazing because we belong to him. We don't need to be smart, great athletes, or good looking. In God's eyes we are treasured and priceless.

**Lord, thank you for loving me more than I can imagine. Thank you for choosing me.**

# Brag about God

*He said to me, "My grace is all you need.*
*My power is strongest when you are weak."*
*So I am very happy to brag about how weak I am.*
*Then Christ's power can rest on me.*

2 CORINTHIANS 12:9 NIRV

Who would want to brag about being the slowest runner on a race team? Or the worst student? Or the least creative artist? It's not very often that we hear people being proud about what they are bad at. We like to show off our skills.

The Bible thinks of bragging differently. It says that we can brag about what we are not good at. Why would it say that? When we are not very good at something, we can see that God is great. We can say, "Wow, there is no way I could have done that all by myself."

*God, shine through the things that I am not good at so I know that you are with me and I can show others how much you care for them.*

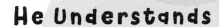

# He Understands

*Have you never heard?*
*Have you never understood?*
*The LORD is the everlasting God,*
*the Creator of all the earth.*
*He never grows weak or weary.*
*No one can measure the depths of his understanding.*

ISAIAH 40:28 NLT

There are times when nothing seems to go your way. Your friends get mad at you for something stupid, your mom decides you have to clean your room when you don't have time, or rain keeps you inside for days. Even when no one seems to listen to us, we are never alone.

God knows exactly what we are going through and he understands. He will never get tired of helping us.

*Oh, God, I am so glad that you understand me. You created me, you know me better than anyone else, and you love me more than I can imagine.*

# Hope in God

*So, Lord, where do I put my hope?*
*My only hope is in you.*
PSALM 39:7 NLT

Would you put an apple in the toaster, or some honey on your toothbrush? Would you put your shoes in the dishwasher, or your brush in the oven? No! You've got to put things in the right place.

The Bible says that the right place for hope is in Jesus. Hope is all about believing in the best for your future, and Jesus is the only one who is going to give you the very best future. So hope in Jesus!

**Lord, today I choose to put my hope in you.**
**You give me everything I need.**

# In His Image

*People will be harder to find than pure gold.*
*There will be fewer people than there is*
*fine gold in Ophir.*

ISAIAH 13:12 ICB

What do you think you have that costs the most money? Is it your parents' car, or the house you live in? Maybe you have a piggy bank with a lot of money in it! If we asked the God what is worth the most, he would say, "You!"

Today you may feel unnoticed and not cared for by anyone. God created you as an amazing human, and you are worth more than fine gold. Believe it!

*Lord, thank you for creating me in your*
*image with no price tag high enough to*
*match my worth. Thank you that I am*
*like gold to you.*

# My Guide

*Then I will lead the blind along a way they never knew.*
*I will guide them along paths they have not known.*
*I will make the darkness become light for them.*
*And I will make the rough ground smooth.*
*These are the things I will do.*
*I will not leave my people.*

ISAIAH 42:16 ICB

Have you ever done a trust walk? One person who is able to see the path ahead has to guide their blindfolded friend around obstacles in order for them to arrive safely to the finish line.

Our walk with God is very similar. God knows what lies ahead. If we listen carefully to his voice, he will lead us in the right direction. God always wants to be trusted. It is up to us to learn to know his voice.

**Thank you, Lord, for always walking with me. Keep me close to you so that I can know you more and continue to hear your voice.**

# Put on Your Belt

*So stand strong, with the belt of truth tied around your waist. And on your chest wear the protection of right living.*

EPHESIANS 6:14 ICB

There is power in truth, but the enemy will always try and lead us away from the truth. Wearing the belt of truth helps us to figure out what is real.

Have you put on your belt of truth today? Spend some time in God's Word and you will find a lot of truth in there. Rely on God and stand firm in the truth!

*Lord, I am so grateful that you have provided a way for me to figure out what is true. I put on the belt of truth this morning and look forward to a day of joy.*

# Slipping

*I cried out, "I am slipping!"*
*but your unfailing love, O LORD, supported me.*
*When doubts filled my mind,*
*your comfort gave me renewed hope and cheer.*
PSALM 94:18-19 NLT

If you know what snow is like, you will know that you can slip on it pretty easily. You can be walking one minute and then falling on the ground the next.

Life can sometimes give us hard things that make us feel like we are on slippery snow. Without God's help, we will fall over. Satan's plan for us is to slip and fall into anger, fear, and unbelief. Cry out to God this morning; hang on to him tightly, and he will keep you from falling.

**Lord, thank you for giving me your hand and helping me every step of the way.**

# God of All Comfort

*Praise be to the God and Father of our Lord Jesus Christ. God is the Father who is full of mercy. And he is the God of all comfort.*

2 Corinthians 1:3 ICB

Comfort is what we need when sad things happen. We need someone to sit beside us, listen to our story, and give us a big hug. Sometimes we don't have friends and family right next to us, but remember that God is there. You can talk to him whenever you feel like it.

Have a great day today. You have a God who loves you. He cares about you. Let him help you when you are down.

**Father, I give you my worry and ask that you would hold my heart. I begin this day with you right next to me.**

# Wait for the Lord

*I wait for the Lord to help me.*
*I trust his word.*
*I wait for the Lord to help me*
*more than night watchmen wait for the dawn,*
*more than night watchmen wait for the dawn.*

PSALM 130:5-6 ICB

Does it seem like forever until your next birthday? You might have one coming up, but once it is over you have to wait a whole year until it comes around again. Waiting can be boring. It takes so long, but it is always worth it.

God even asks us to wait. He doesn't always answer our prayer straight away or answer it exactly how we ask. In time, our answer will come and it will be worth it.

*Lord, please help me to be patient as I wait for you to move in my life. You work everything together for my good. I trust you to do what is best.*

246

# Looking at the Heart

*The Lord said to Samuel, "Don't look at how handsome Eliab is. Don't look at how tall he is. I have not chosen him. God does not see the same way people see. People look at the outside of a person, but the Lord looks at the heart."*

1 SAMUEL 16:7 ICB

When you see yourself in the mirror, do you like what you see? Some of us wish for nicer hair, or brighter eyes, or a straighter smile. We can spend a long time wondering how others look at us, or comparing ourselves to movie stars or even our closest friends.

It doesn't matter how good you look on the outside, it only matters how you are doing on the inside. God sees the parts of you that others don't. He sees it all, he sees your heart, and he loves you completely.

*Jesus, help me see myself the way you see me. Remind me of how you look at the beauty of my heart.*

# Be Brave

*We have this hope, so we are very brave.*
2 CORINTHIANS 3:12 ICB

Imagine you were up on a really high mountain and had to jump all the way to the bottom. It would be too scary, right? But imagine if you were told that there was a huge fluffy landing all the way around the mountain and especially at the bottom. You would jump if you knew it would be fun!

The Bible says that having hope makes us bold. It's like that big fluffy landing that makes you not afraid to jump. We have hope that one day we will be in heaven with God and everyone else who has loved him. That can make us joyful and brave.

*Jesus, thank you that I can have boldness because I have hope that you make all things good.*

# Forgive

*"If you forgive others for their sins, your Father in heaven will also forgive you for your sins."*

MATTHEW 6:14 NCV

If someone is mean to us, or hurts us while we are playing, we don't usually want to forgive. Sometimes we want to stay mad because we are still hurting. It can feel good to stay mad at times, even if the person says sorry.

God was hurt by his people because they kept doing wrong things. It hurts him when we sin, but he always forgives us because he loves us so much. We need to try to be like God toward others. Ask him to help you forgive like he does.

*Jesus, remind me that you are always kind toward me. Help me to forgive others because I want to be kind too.*

# I Need Grace

> *God continues to give us more grace.*
> *That's why Scripture says,*
> *"God opposes those who are proud.*
> *But he gives grace to those who are humble."*
> JAMES 4:6 ESV

If you were playing a game with friends and someone got bossy, telling everyone that you had to play by their rules, how would you feel? Would you want to do it their way? Now think of someone who kindly says that there might be a better way to play the game. You would probably listen.

Jesus wants to listen to people when they ask him with a good heart. If you try to tell him to do it your way, it doesn't show that you care about what is best. Being humble means listening to Jesus. He will give you grace.

*Jesus, thank you that you created me to need you. Help me to know that you always have the best way.*

# Welcome!

*Welcome one another as Christ has welcomed you,
for the glory of God.*
ROMANS 15:7 ESV

Have you ever been in a class where a new student joined in the middle of the year? Maybe you have been the new person yourself. New people can feel a little lost and not know who to talk to.

The best way to show God's love to the lonely is to open your arms and your heart to them. God never wants us to feel alone. He wants us to know that we are loved and he wants us to show others that they are loved. Welcome new people just like Jesus has welcomed you.

*Lord, help me see and love the lonely like you do. When I'm lonely, help me to feel you with me.*

# Piggy Bank

*How great is the goodness*
*you have stored up for those who fear you.*
*You lavish it on those who come to you for protection,*
*blessing them before the watching world.*

PSALM 31:19 NLT

Do you own a piggy bank, or know what a piggy bank is? They usually have a coin slot to put your money in, little by little. Over time, the piggy bank gets more and more full. If you could wait until it was completely full, you would count a lot of money in it!

The goodness that God gives us is like a coin in a piggy bank. God just keeps putting more goodness into our lives, until one day we have so much goodness that it spills out to the people around us.

**God, your blessings are all around me, thank you for your goodness that overflows in me.**

# Not Just Mr. Fix It

*Enter his gates with thanksgiving
and his courts with praise;
give thanks to him and praise his name.*

PSALM 100:4 NIV

How do you ask God for things? Do you complain about what you don't have, or tell him exactly what you want? Sometimes we look at God as our magic guy who will pay for everything, fix everything, and make sure we have exactly what we want.

God wants us to tell him what we need, what we are afraid of, and how we need help, but he also wants us to tell him when we are happy, thankful, or amazed. He deserves your thanks, so tell him how grateful you are, today.

**God, I thank you for everything good and right in my life.**

253

# Help Others

*Carry one another's heavy loads.*
*If you do, you will fulfill the law of Christ.*
GALATIANS 6:2 NIRV

Have you ever had to move something that was too heavy to push on your own? You might have needed a friend to come alongside you and help you push it. We all need a little help sometimes.

Do you have a friend that could use a hug, or some kind words? Be a good friend and help because Jesus wants you to show love to others.

*Jesus, help me to show love to those around me. Thank you for my friends!*

# Out of the Gates

*"If the Son sets you free, you will be free indeed."*
JOHN 8:36 NIV

During school, you are not allowed to leave the gates that go around the outside of the school. Once school is finished, you can walk right out of those gates without getting into trouble.

Before Jesus died and rose again, we were like kids inside a school with strict rules. When Jesus died and rose again, it was like we were let out of the gates—we were set free!

**Thank you, Jesus, for rescuing me and setting me free.**

# Surrounded by Gifts

*My God will meet all your needs. He will meet them in keeping with his wonderful riches. These riches come to you because you belong to Christ Jesus.*

PHILIPPIANS 4:19 NIRV

When your mom or dad makes a shopping list, they go around the kitchen and look at what is in the cupboards to see if there is any food that might be missing that the family will need.

God is always checking to see what we need. He gives us what we need and then he gives us extra things—we call these blessings! Blessings could be good health, kind friends, and a happy family, and they are all from God. God shows us that he cares by taking care of our needs.

**Jesus, thank you that you give me all that I need, and often bless me with more!**

# SEPTEMBER

The Lord will keep his promises.
With love he takes care of all he has made.
The Lord helps those
who have been defeated.
He takes care of those who are in trouble.

PSALM 145:13-14 ICB

# Big or Small

*Give all your worries to him, because he cares for you.*
1 PETER 5:7 NCV

We can find a lot to worry about in a day. Will I have enough time to finish my homework? Did I remember to feed the dog? Do my shoes match my outfit?

None of these worries are too small for God. Big or small he cares. We can forget just how much he cares when we focus on our worries instead of his blessings. He gives us promises like our verse today to remind us that we are his when it seems like we have a lot to worry about.

**God, whenever I begin to worry, about tiny things or big things, help me to tell you how I feel and then to trust that you will take care of them.**

# Best Relationships

*Whoever spends time with wise people
will become wise.
But whoever makes friends with fools will suffer.*
PROVERBS 13:20 ICB

When a rotten apple is put with other apples, the rot in the apple can make the other apples start to go bad as well. That's what it can be like to hang out with people that don't make very good decisions.

Do you have some friends in your life that you think make really good decisions? Are there friends in your life that you think make bad decisions? We have all kinds of friends, but the Bible says that it's pretty smart to stick close to the friends that do good because it helps us to stay good as well.

**Dear Jesus, thank you for the gift of friendship, help me to stick close to my friends who are wise.**

# My Healer

*O Lord my God, I cried to you for help,
and you have healed me.*

Psalm 30:2 esv

When people are sick, they usually need help. Do you remember times when you have been sick? You don't have much energy to get out of bed, or to eat food, or to play. An adult will have to stay home and help you. They will keep you warm and bring you food and water.

God cares when we are sick. He wants us to ask him for help. God made our bodies and he knows how to heal our bodies. He also made wonderful helpers for us. The people that care for you when you are sick are God's way of helping you. Thank him for his help today.

*Jesus, thank you that you can heal me and that you help me when I am sick.*

# God Answers

*When you ask, you must believe and not doubt, because the one who doubts is like a wave of the sea, blown and tossed by the wind.*

JAMES 1:6 NIV

Have you ever thrown a ball or a stick into the ocean and watched it bob around all over the place in the waves? God says that when we stop believing in him or in his goodness, we are like that stick, getting twirled around everywhere, not knowing where we will end up.

When you believe, you are more like a strong tree in the ground, you are someone who knows that God is good, that God loves you, and that God will answer you. Believe in God's answers today.

*Jesus, I believe in you. I believe that you love me, that you care for me, and that you will answer me.*

# More Faith

*Hope deferred makes the heart sick,
but a dream fulfilled is a tree of life.*
PROVERBS 13:12 NLT

How would you feel if you were waiting for your turn on the swing and the person on the swing stayed on it for a really long time? What if they said, "Okay, give me one more minute," and then they took five more minutes? That's the kind of waiting that isn't very good!

God won't make us wait for wrong reasons. Sometimes we have to wait for good reasons, but he isn't trying to make us frustrated or upset. God gives you great dreams for your life and he wants all of the right things to work out for you.

*Jesus, thank you that you give me hopes and dreams for a beautiful future and that I can trust that you want the very best for me.*

# Hard to Love

*Dear friends, let us continue to love one another, for love comes from God. Anyone who loves is a child of God and knows God.*

1 JOHN 4:7 NLT

Can you think of anyone that you find hard to love? Maybe there is a mean person at school, or someone you know that brags all the time. There might even be someone in your family that you always fight with.

The good news is that you don't have to love people all by yourself. The Bible says that love comes from God. The next time you think it is too hard to love someone, just ask God to give you his love for them.

*God, I need your love right now. There are some kids that I find really hard to love, but I know that I can show them love with your help.*

# Be Courageous!

*"Remember that I commanded you to be strong and brave. So don't be afraid. The Lord your God will be with you everywhere you go."*

JOSHUA 1:9 ICB

We all need courage. It doesn't matter if we're young or old, tall or short, confident or shy. We could need courage to say sorry, to perform a song, or to stand up for what is right. We need courage in the most boring parts of life and in the most exciting parts.

Whatever we do, we don't have to be afraid because God is with us. We can be brave because we know that he helps us with everything and he is right by our side, all the time.

***Jesus, show me how to stand strong and to be brave. Thank you for being my strength.***

# Full of Peace

*"Peace I leave with you; my peace I give you. I do not give to you as the world gives. Do not let your hearts be troubled and do not be afraid."*

JOHN 14:27 NIV

Have you ever seen a baby sleeping? Have you been outside and realized that everything was quiet? What about a time when you were quietly drawing and nobody was around to mess things up? These are moments of peace.

God loves peace! He loves it so much that he gives you peace. Sometimes things are too busy or too noisy or too scary. In those times, ask God for his peace in your heart; that is what he wants to give you.

***Thank you, Jesus, for your gift of peace, I am so thankful that you settle and calm my heart.***

# Accepted

*"Those the Father has given me will come to me, and I will never reject them."*

JOHN 6:37 NLT

Competitions are usually fun, but they can also make you nervous. If you don't win or get a prize, you can be a bit embarrassed or feel rejected.

When it comes to God, there is no competition. He accepts everyone just as they are because he loves us all the same. He created you to be different than everyone else, and he loves that you are different. Remember that you will always be accepted by God.

**Thank you, God, that you love me for exactly who I am. I am accepted by you because you created me and think that I am awesome.**

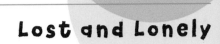

# Lost and Lonely

*He saw the crowds of people and felt sorry
for them because they were worried and helpless.
They were like sheep without a shepherd.*

MATTHEW 9:36 ICB

Have you ever been lost in a store and had someone come and help you? They might have seen you crying or looking all alone, and even though they don't know you, they wanted to help.

Jesus felt like this when he saw people around him who were hurting. He feels sad for people that are lost and lonely. That's why he always wants to help us and others. He cares so much that he helps us to find our way.

***Jesus, thank you that you care enough to help me when I am lost and lonely. Help me to be like you and care for others, too.***

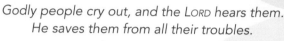

# Help Me!

*Godly people cry out, and the LORD hears them.*
*He saves them from all their troubles.*
PSALM 34:17 NIRV

Have you heard the saying, "There's no such thing as a stupid question"? It's important to ask for help when you don't understand something. That is how we learn.

God knows that we need to learn about life and about how to follow. That's why he says that when we ask him a question, or ask him for help, he hears us and chooses to answer us. He loves your questions, and he wants you to ask him for help.

**Jesus, thank you that I can always ask you for help. Please help me today, when things get hard, and save me from any trouble.**

# God's Love

*I pray that you and all God's holy people will have the
power to understand the greatness of Christ's love.
I pray that you can understand how wide and how
long and how high and how deep that love is.
Christ's love is greater than any person can ever know.
But I pray that you will be able to know that love.
Then you can be filled with the fullness of God.*
EPHESIANS 3:18-19 ICB

Do you understand how big the ocean is? Do you
know how deep it is, or how big it is? How long would
it take you to travel from one side of the sea to the
other side? When you think about the ocean, it seems
way too big to understand!

Jesus' love is like the ocean. It's just way too big
and deep to even understand. But just like the ocean,
it is real and it is always going to be there.
So, get into his love; it is beautiful!

**God, open my heart today to see just
how beautiful and big and deep your
love is for me.**

# Doing Good

*Since future victory is sure, be strong and steady, always abounding in the Lord's work, for you know that nothing you do for the Lord is ever wasted as it would be if there were no resurrection.*

1 CORINTHIANS 15:58 TLB

When you decide to share your cookie with your sister, when you help your dad set the table, when you stop to give a teammate a hand—God notices. He notices all the good things you do, even if they seem small.

The Bible says that nothing that you do for God is ever wasted, because doing good things always shows others that there is love is the world, and this gives us all hope.

***Jesus, sometimes I wonder if anyone notices some of the kind and right things that I do. Thank you that you do.***

# The Light

*"I am the light of the world. Whoever follows me will not walk in darkness, but will have the light of life."*
JOHN 8:12 ESV

Imagine a world where it was always nighttime. It wouldn't be as warm, you wouldn't see colors brightly, and you might just be sleepier! A world without light would look and feel different.

When Jesus came, he said that he was the light. Things look and feel a whole lot better when Jesus is near. Let him show you his light so you can have a beautiful life.

*Jesus, thank you for your presence that is continuous light when darkness threatens to overtake me. You are my rescuer, my Savior, and the one who loves me perfectly through it all.*

# Being Like Jesus

*"The greatest love a person can show
is to die for his friends."*

JOHN 15:13 ICB

Who would you want to be like when you grow up? You might admire your teacher, doctor, or maybe a famous singer. We want to be like the people that have done awesome things.

Remember that Jesus has done the most amazing thing. He gave up his own life so the whole world could live eternally. He loves everyone all the same. He walked on water, raised people from the dead, and healed the hurting. Being like Jesus would be the greatest thing you could ever do!

*Jesus, thank you that you gave up
your life for me. Help me to be
someone who loves people
that much too.*

# Broken Bones

*He heals the brokenhearted.*
*He bandages their wounds.*
PSALM 147:3 ICB

Have you ever had a broken bone, or had someone at school break an arm or leg? The broken bone takes time heal. A doctor will usually put a cast on it to make sure that it stays in the same place so it can grow back together.

Our hearts can be like a broken bone. We talk about being hurt when people do wrong things to us. Jesus wants you to know that he will heal your heart, just like those bones that heal. He can help you and he wants to make you better.

**Thank you, Jesus, that you care so much about me that you take the time to heal anything in me that is hurting.**

273

# No Conditions

*Let us, then, feel free to come before God's throne. Here there is grace. And we can receive mercy and grace to help us when we need it.*

HEBREWS 4:16 ICB

It is hard to believe that love will remain forever. The love that God the Father has for us comes without rules. There is absolutely nothing we can do or say that will take away his love.

Even though we sometimes make bad choices, we can still go to God for forgiveness. He will always welcome us when we are sorry. In fact, he says to be bold about asking for forgiveness. Ask him for his grace, and he will say yes!

***Thank you, Jesus, that I can be so sure that you will forgive me. I ask for your forgiveness right now, and know that you welcome me with love.***

# Joy Is Coming!

*"It is the same with you. Now you are sad.
But I will see you again and you will be happy.
And no one will take away your joy."*
JOHN 16:22 ICB

There are times when we are separated from our parents. It might be when you go to school, or a summer camp. Your parents might go on vacation or a work trip and leave you with other people to care for you.

You might feel sad when they leave, but every day that passes means that you are one day closer to seeing them again. When the time comes, it's exciting to see them again and you feel happy. It will feel even better than this when we see Jesus!

***Jesus, thank you that one day we will see you again, and it will make us so very happy!***

# Strong and Sure

*When I am afraid, I will put my confidence in you.
Yes, I will trust the promises of God. And since I am
trusting him, what can mere man do to me?*
PSALM 56:3-4 TLB

Have you ever seen a bird in a cage with a cat sitting outside watching the bird? If there was no cage, the bird would be really afraid, but the bird knows that it is safe inside the cage.

We can feel as strong and sure as that little bird because we have the best protection of all—Jesus Christ. He is faithful, and you can trust him to take care of you.

***Jesus, when I am afraid, I know that you will comfort all my fears. Let me feel safe and secure, knowing you care for me.***

# A Beautiful Gift

*No matter what happens, always be thankful, for this is God's will for you who belong to Christ Jesus.*
1 Thessalonians 5:18 TLB

It is easy to be thankful when everything in life is going well. But it can be hard to be thankful when life is hard. We always have a choice. We can be grumpy when things are going wrong, or we can choose thankfulness.

When we choose to be thankful, we see all the good things, rather than all the bad. The next time you want to complain about dinner, be thankful that you have food. When you are mad with a friend, be thankful that God gave you friends. When you are feeling sick, be thankful that Jesus has forgiven you. Being thankful is good for you!

*Thank you, Jesus, for all the wonderful things in my life. Help me to change my bad mood into a good mood because I am thankful!*

# On Your Side

*Surely God is my salvation;*
*I will trust and not be afraid.*
*The LORD, the LORD himself,*
*is my strength and my defense;*
*he has become my salvation.*

ISAIAH 12:2 NIV

When a soccer player scores a goal, or a basketball player gets a ball in the net, they are celebrated for earning points for the team. But that soccer player or that basketball player didn't just get that goal by themselves. The rest of the team would have been working hard to make that happen.

In the same way, God works with us and for us, so that we can be winners. You don't have to do great things on your own, you don't have to be afraid or worried because God is on your side.

**Lord, thank you that I have you on my team to support and help me every day!**

# You Will Make It

*When you pass through the waters, I will be with you.*
*When you cross rivers, you will not drown.*
*When you walk through fire, you will not be burned.*
*The flames will not hurt you.*

Isaiah 43:2 icb

Do you know the story of Shadrach, Meshach, and Abednego? They were three young guys who didn't bow down to the idol as their king had demanded. Instead, they worshipped God, so the king threw them into the fire. The miracle was that they did not get burned at all, and everyone believed in the one true God because of their faith.

You can have faith like these guys. Sometimes you don't want to have bad or sad things happen to you, but you can believe that God will rescue you. When God saves you from hard times, other people will know that you have an awesome God!

**Jesus, I pray that through my faith, people would see that you are awesome.**

# Made Clean

*O loving and kind God, have mercy. Have pity upon me and take away the awful stain of my transgressions. Oh, wash me, cleanse me from this guilt. Let me be pure again.*

PSALM 51:1-2 TLB

Nobody is perfect. We all make mistakes. The really great news is that God loves us all anyway; it doesn't matter what we have done.

King David made some terrible mistakes, probably worse than you would ever make. David knew that he could turn to his Father in heaven and be made clean. We can do the same. Our incredible God shows us grace when we least deserve it. We only need to ask for it.

**Lord, I ask for your forgiveness. I ask for my sins to be washed away and for my heart to become clean again.**

# Rest

*"Come to me, all of you who are tired and have heavy loads. I will give you rest. Accept my work and learn from me. I am gentle and humble in spirit. And you will find rest for your souls. The work that I ask you to accept is easy. The load I give you to carry is not heavy."*

MATTHEW 11:28-30 ICB

Do you often get home from school, or from sports practice, and just flop on the floor? It can be so tiring! You just want to take off your shoes, jacket, and bag, and lie down.

Sometimes our heart feels heavy and tired with things that we worry or feel sad about. God promises to take those feelings away, just like taking off your bag and shoes. He wants your heart and mind to find rest in him.

**Jesus, thank you for taking away the things that worry me. Thank you that you can give my heart peace and that you can give my mind a rest.**

# Good Friends

*A real friend sticks closer than a brother.*
PROVERBS 18:24 NLT

Sometimes all we want is to be with a good friend and talk or play. We want to share our joys and our worries with someone who really cares. We want to enjoy just hanging out. Everyone needs a friend like that.

Just like you need a good friend, so do other people. Are you being a good friend? God wants you to stick close to your good friends, to care for them and to stick up for them. God made friendship for good.

**God, I am thankful for all my friends.**
**Help me to be a really good friend today.**

# Rewards with Work

*We believe it is through the grace of our Lord Jesus that we are saved.*
ACTS 15:11 NIV

Do you get rewards for doing good things and working hard? Do you get stars on your chart, special time with your parents, or maybe even money?

Rewards are great, but that's not how you get into heaven. You don't have to do anything to be accepted by God; you just have to believe in Jesus. It can seem a little too easy, but that is what God's grace is all about. It's his gift to you.

**Thank you, Jesus, that I don't have to be perfect all the time to have eternal life with you.**

# Cuddly Blanket

*Blessed are those who are sad.*
*They will be comforted.*
MATTHEW 5:4 NIRV

On a really cold night you might need to wrap yourself up in a really big cozy blanket. Do you have a favorite blanket to keep you warm? A blanket helps you to feel comfortable when everything outside is cold.

God knows that sometimes we are really sad or upset and he wants to make us feel okay in those times. Just like a big blanket, God covers our hearts in his love and makes us feel better again.

*Jesus, thank you that when I am upset, you comfort me. Help me to know that you are right there beside me when I need you.*

# Seasons

*"God blesses you who are hungry now,*
*for you will be satisfied.*
*God blesses you who weep now,*
*for in due time you will laugh."*

LUKE 6:21 NLT

Do you ever find yourself wishing that one season would end so that you could go into the next one? Maybe you are waiting for summer, when you can go outside and spend a lot of time in the water. You could be waiting for fall because that is when your sports team starts games again. You might even be waiting for winter so that you can play in the snow.

It's good to know that cool things happen in every season. God says that however you feel, there will be a time when those feelings come to an end, and you will be blessed with different feelings.

***Jesus, I am thankful that you created all the different seasons that I go through in life. Help me to remember that there are good times ahead.***

# Never Leaving

*The LORD himself goes before you and will be with you; he will never leave you nor forsake you. Do not be afraid; do not be discouraged.*

DEUTERONOMY 31:8 NIV

On a dark and cloudy day, you might feel cold and wet. Sometimes you can't see the sun because there are too many clouds. But that doesn't mean the sun isn't there! If you were to take a plane right through those clouds, you would see the sun shining as brightly as ever.

Sometimes in our hearts and minds we feel dark and gloomy. You might not think that Jesus is around. Just like the sun, Jesus is always there, and he is always for you. Remember that he is just a prayer away.

*Jesus, I need your light in my life. When things get too hard, please remind me that you are here. Thank you that you never leave me.*

# New Life

*"What I'm about to tell you is true. Unless a grain of wheat falls to the ground and dies, it remains only one seed. But if it dies, it produces many seeds."*

JOHN 12:24 NIRV

Have you ever seen a gigantic tree and wondered how it got so big? Have you ever thought about how that tree began? It started as a tiny seed that had fallen from another tree.

Jesus used this picture to describe what happened when he died. He fell to the ground like that tiny seed, but something so incredible happened after he died and rose again. He saved people from sin, and now we have eternal life in him. Amazing!

**Thank you, Jesus, for loving me enough to die for me. In that place, new life begins. Thank you for bringing me to new life!**

# OCTOBER

"For I know the plans I have for you,"
says the LORD.
"They are plans for good
and not for disaster,
to give you a future and a hope."

JEREMIAH 29:11 NLT

# The Best Answer

*Wait for the LORD;*
*be strong, and let your heart take courage;*
*wait for the LORD!*
PSALM 27:14 NRSV

When you are playing hide and seek, you have to wait for someone to find you. You might have hidden really well, but you know that after a few minutes you will probably be found.

Sometimes we have to wait for answers from God. We know that it doesn't happen straight away. The Bible says that we can believe that when we wait for God to answer us, he will give us the very best answer.

**Thank you, Jesus, that you don't stay silent forever. You answer me when I need you the most. Help me to be patient.**

289

# Patience!

*If we hope for what we do not see,*
*we wait for it with patience.*
ROMANS 8:25 ESV

When you fall over and scrape your hands and knees, or if you have ever cut yourself with something sharp, you know that the scratches heal. You also know that they don't heal straight away. The body takes a little bit of time to fix itself.

Waiting for God's help or answer is a little bit like waiting for a scratch to heal. You know for sure that it will get better and it will be okay in the end, but you do have to wait. Be sure of God's goodness for you today, and be patient while you wait.

**Jesus, I am so grateful that you give me hope and peace while I am waiting for you.**

# I Am Enough

*"Before I formed you in your mother's body I chose you.*
*Before you were born I set you apart to serve me.*
*I appointed you to be a prophet to the nations."*

JEREMIAH 1:5 NIRV

It's amazing to think that before you were born, God knew you. Nobody else knew you before you were born, not even your parents. But God did because he planned your life right from the tiny beginning of it.

Your parents are proud of you and they love you just because you belong to them. Imagine how much more God loves you and is so very proud of you because you belong to him. He has great things planned for your life.

*Jesus, when I feel small, help me to know in my heart that I am yours. Thank you that you will help me to do things in my life that I never thought possible.*

# Joyful Music

*During danger he will keep me safe in his shelter.*
*He will hide me in his Holy Tent.*
*Or he will keep me safe on a high mountain.*
*My head is higher*
*than my enemies around me.*
*I will offer joyful sacrifices in his Holy Tent.*
*I will sing and praise the Lord.*
*Lord, hear me when I call.*
*Be kind and answer me.*

PSALM 27:5-7 ICB

Do you play an instrument, or would you like to play an instrument? What kind of music do you like to listen to?

God gave us music as a gift, it can help us in times of trouble. When we feel annoyed, sad, or upset, music can help bring joy to your heart. The next time you feel like you might get into trouble with your attitude, give it to God and play some music. Let his gift of music help you find joy.

**Jesus, when times are hard, help me to choose joy. Let the joy that you give me be a witness and a testimony to the love you have for me.**

# Most of All

*Most of all, love one another deeply.*
*Love erases many sins by forgiving them.*

1 PETER 4:8 NIRV

Love is one of those things that we just can't measure. We either love or we don't. We can't choose to love those around us just a little.

Loving is doing what is best for others. This doesn't always feel good, and it can be hard, especially if someone has done something unkind toward us. In the end, love feels like the best thing to do. When you forgive someone, you make them feel better. This is just what Jesus has done for you. He forgives you because he wants you to know that you are loved, no matter what.

*Jesus, continue to teach me how to love with all my heart. Help me to love others the way you do.*

# Money Monster

*Keep your lives free from the love of money. And be*
*satisfied with what you have. God has said,*
*"I will never leave you;*
*I will never abandon you."*

HEBREWS 13:5 ICB

You can get money for doing jobs around the house, or sometimes for your birthday, or maybe a relative sends you money in a card. What do you do with your money when you get it? Do you save it, or do you like to spend it?

Money is a great thing to have, but the Bible warns us not to love it too much. What usually happens when people get a lot of money is that they become greedy. That means they want more and more and more, and they don't like to share. Money is to be used for good and not evil, and to remember that Jesus will always make sure we have what we need.

**Thank you, Jesus, that you have given me such a beautiful life. Thank you that you are truly all I need.**

# Ask for Help

*I asked the L*ORD *for help, and he answered me.*
*He saved me from all that I feared.*
*Those who go to him for help are happy,*
*and they are never disgraced.*

PSALM 34:4-5 NCV

It is okay to ask for help. We can't do everything by ourselves, and God never wanted us to be alone. We need food to keep us healthy, clothes to keep us warm, and a roof over our heads to keep us safe. We need friends and family to keep us happy.

Asking for help, from God or a friend, is a good thing. It gives us the opportunity to learn and grow.

*Jesus, thank you that I don't always have to know everything. Help me to know when I am in need and to accept help from others.*

# Thankfulness

*Every good action and every perfect gift is from God. These good gifts come down from the Creator of the sun, moon, and stars. God does not change like their shifting shadows.*

JAMES 1:17 ICB

Every year we look forward to special days like birthdays because we might get something that we really want. On days like this, we may forget to realize what we already have.

It's good to remember to be thankful for everything. When we start to think of all the things we can be thankful for, we realize how many things God has blessed us with. We see all the wonderful ways that Jesus provides and cares for us.

***Thank you, Lord, that you love to surprise me daily. Remind me that you have given me many good things. Help me to have a thankful heart.***

# Carried Close

*He takes care of people like a shepherd.*
*He gathers them like lambs in his arms*
*and carries them close to him.*
ISAIAH 40:11 NCV

When a small child or baby animal is afraid, it will always look for its parents. It needs to be close to them to feel safe and protected.

Jesus is our heavenly parent. When we are afraid and need help, the Bible says that he is like our shepherd. He lets us come close to him so we can feel that he is near, and know that we are loved and protected.

***Thank you, Jesus, that you are my shepherd and want to keep me close to you. Help me to come close to you every day.***

# Praise Always

*Let everything alive give praises to the Lord!*
*You praise him!*
*Hallelujah!*

PSALM 150:6 TLB

Have you heard a bird sing, or seen a tree wave around in the wind like it is dancing? All of God's creation has ways of praising him, and they all seem to be like a song. When living things are happy or glad, they make noise, they dance, they share love.

What can you do to praise God? You can sing, you can dance, you can laugh, you can love. Everything alive praises God somehow, so find a way to praise him, today!

*Jesus, may I always praise you no matter how my days are going. Let me never forget to remind myself of how good you are.*

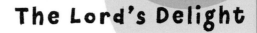

# The Lord's Delight

*The Lord is pleased with his people.*
*He saves those who are not proud.*

PSALM 149:4 ICB

You might have a cute baby brother or sister, or maybe you know of a cute baby at school or church. Don't you just want to look at them, play with them, and give them a big hug?

That is how Jesus feels about you! He loves everything about you; he loves to spend time with you and meet your every need. He will go to the ends of the earth to protect you. He is your loving and faithful Father who delights in you.

**God, I am amazed that you feel such joy when you look at me. Thank you that I am yours.**

# Powerful

*I will go before you.*
*And I will make the mountains flat.*
*I will break down the bronze gates of the cities.*
*I will cut through the iron bars on the gates.*
*I will give you the wealth that is stored away.*
*And I will give you hidden riches.*
*I will do this so you will know I am the Lord.*
*I, the God of Israel, call you by name.*

ISAIAH 45:2-3 ICB

Think of the most powerful thing that exists. You might be thinking of a huge mountain, crashing waves, a roaring lion, or maybe even the tallest tower in the world. Not many things can stand in the way of something that powerful.

God is the only thing more powerful than anything you can think of. He can smash down gates and cut through iron. Wow! Isn't it amazing to know that this powerful God does this so he can give you treasures and riches? What a mighty God you have on your side.

**Powerful God, thank you that your promises give me strength and courage in every situation.**

# Victory over Sin

*You are tempted in the same way all other human beings are. God is faithful. He will not let you be tempted any more than you can take. But when you are tempted, God will give you a way out. Then you will be able to deal with it.*

1 CORINTHIANS 10:13 NIRV

Have you ever done something wrong and then worried that you will never get it right? Maybe you have even thought you were the worst kid in your family or class. The truth is, God sees every wrong thing the same. You are not better or worse than anyone, God just wants to help you to make things right.

God does not let you keep sinning. He gives you the strength each time to get better and better at doing the right thing. You just have to ask him to help you and he will.

*Jesus, thank you that you help me to get things right. Thank you for giving me the courage to see every day as a brand new day.*

# Wasted Worry

*"Don't worry. Don't say, 'What will we eat?' Or, 'What will we drink?' Or, 'What will we wear?' People who are ungodly run after all those things. Your Father who is in heaven knows that you need them. But put God's kingdom first. Do what he wants you to do. Then all those things will also be given to you."*

MATTHEW 6:31-33 NIRV

If you play board games, you will know that there is a start and a finish to every game. As you play a game, there are things that get in the way of you finishing, like not answering a question right, or having to skip a turn.

What if you spent the whole game worrying about what could go wrong. It wouldn't be a very enjoyable game for you. God says that life is like that. You can't keep worrying about what might go wrong. To enjoy life, you need to trust God and look to the finish line—one day you will get to that treasure!

*Jesus, help me keep my eyes and heart centered on you and not to worry about things that I can't control.*

# What Next?

*Show me the right path, O LORD;*
*point out the road for me to follow.*
*Lead me by your truth and teach me,*
*for you are the God who saves me.*
*All day long I put my hope in you.*
PSALM 25:4-5 NLT

There will be so many choices to make as you grow up. Some of them are small like what color backpack to get for school. Others will be big like what college to go to, or what job to work at.

We can be wise when we make decisions because we trust in God. God is the best teacher and will show you the right steps, one at a time. He even says that he will lead the way, and because he is in front, you don't need to worry. So enjoy following Jesus!

*Jesus, I choose to follow you today, and*
*every day. I trust that you know where*
*we are going and I look forward*
*to what life will bring.*

# Read the Bible

*All Scripture is inspired by God and is useful
for teaching, for showing people what is wrong
in their lives, for correcting faults,
and for teaching how to live right.*

2 TIMOTHY 3:16 NCV

The Bible seems boring sometimes. But that's only because we don't read it enough. It's hard to read your Bible when you have other books to read, games to play, and friends to hang out with.

The Bible has so many great stories in it. It also has some encouraging words to make you feel better when you are down. It has good promises about your future. It teaches you how to live a better life. The Bible is a good book, so make it a fun book by getting into it.

*God, thank you so much for giving us the Bible. Thank you that I have a Bible and that I can read it. Help me to find truth, hope, and fun in your Word, and to read it more.*

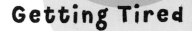

# Getting Tired

*Let us not become weary in doing good,*
*for at the proper time we will reap*
*a harvest if we do not give up.*

GALATIANS 6:9 NIV

When you have run a really long race, you usually get very tired. Sometimes you might have stopped to walk when you were feeling like you just couldn't keep going.

Following God isn't always easy. In fact, he tells us that the road can be difficult. But living for him is worth every last ounce of our energy. Others might be quick to tell us that it's not worth it, but Jesus says to carry on. Be strong. Keep going. Don't give up.

***God, when I think I might have to give up,***
***please give me the strength to keep going.***

# Watching Over You

*He will not let you be defeated.*
*He who guards you never sleeps.*
PSALM 121:3 ICB

Do you know the story of the BFG? He's a big friendly giant who blows dreams into people's ears when they are sleeping. He is the only one awake when everyone else is asleep.

Of course, that story is made up, but did you know there is a true story about someone who never sleeps? The Bible says that God never sleeps, so that means that he is able to watch over you every single moment of the day—and night!

***Jesus, thank you that I can always count on your constant presence in my life. Thank you that I can trust you completely.***

# Created for a Purpose

*We know that in all things God works for the good of those who love him, who have been called according to his purpose.*

ROMANS 8:28 NIV

What do you dream of doing as you get older? Do you think of a job that you want to have? Do you think of taking care of your own children? Maybe you think of exciting places you want to visit.

God has a purpose for your life. He wants you to do things you love, and he wants you to do those while you are loving and following him. You might not know what your purpose in life is, but you will find it when you choose to love God with all of your heart.

***Jesus, when I feel lost, let me find purpose in simply loving and serving you.***

# Free to Live

*We have freedom now because Christ made us free.*
*So stand strong. Do not change and go back*
*into the slavery of the law.*

GALATIANS 5:1 ICB

Imagine if you had been captured and sent to jail. It would make you so happy if someone found a way to rescue you and get you out of jail. You would run free and never go near the jail again.

Jesus rescued us from our sin and we have a brand new start because he has forgiven us. When we keep feeling guilty about our sin, it's like going back to the jail and putting the chains back on our hands and feet. God wants us to feel free and good about his forgiveness, so stay free!

***Jesus, thank you for giving me a brand new life in you. Thank you for freeing me from guilt and giving me a life full of grace.***

# Say Yes

*The yes to all of God's promises is in Christ, and through Christ we say yes to the glory of God.*

2 CORINTHIANS 1:20 NCV

We hear a lot of no's in our life. No, you can't go out with your friends. No, you can't have another piece of cake. No you can't bring your new toy to school. It's pretty great when we get to hear yes, isn't it?

God made a lot of good promises. He said that we would be forgiven. He said that we would be part of his family. He said that we would have eternal life. The best thing is, that he made all of these promises come true by sending Jesus to us. All you need to do is to say yes to Jesus and all of God's promises will come true in your life.

*God, I say yes, right now, to your promises for my life. I say yes to your forgiveness, yes to being a part of your family, and yes to eternal life!*

# Copycat

*Don't live the way this world lives. Let your way of thinking be completely changed. Then you will be able to test what God wants for you. And you will agree that what he wants is right. His plan is good and pleasing and perfect.*

ROMANS 12:2 NIRV

Stop copying me. *Stop copying me.* No really stop copying me! *No really stop copying me!* We have all been a part of this game. It can be either funny or annoying depending which side you are on.

God wants us to copy him. He doesn't get annoyed when we follow right behind him because he knows the best thing for us is to copy what he does.

**Thank you, Father, that you are good and loving and right. Help me to copy you every day.**

# The Body

*Each of us has one body with many parts. And the parts do not all have the same purpose. So also we are many persons. But in Christ we are one body. And each part of the body belongs to all the other parts.*

ROMANS 12:4-5 NIRV

Can your eyes listen to sounds? Can your ears talk? Can you walk on your nose? No! Your body is made up of different parts, and each part of the body does something special to help you move, grow, and live.

Jesus says that God's family is like a body. We are all different parts and he doesn't want us to be exactly like each other. The best way to make God's family work, is for you to just be you. Everyone needs you to do your special part.

**Father, thank you that you have made me different to everyone else. Help me to remember how important it is to just be me!**

# Weight of Worry

*Worry makes a person feel as if he is carrying a heavy load.*
*But a kind word cheers up a person.*
PROVERBS 12:25 ICB

We often find ourselves thinking too much about the wrong things. We might start to worry about what we look like, or about playing a new sport. We might wonder if we will ever be good enough for the school musical, or think too much about being popular in class. These kinds of thoughts can make us feel nervous.

Isn't it great when your parents or good friends tell you that everything is going to be okay? They might make you laugh or tell you that you don't need to worry. Good words are good for everyone and they need to be shared!

*God, when I begin to feel nervous, I pray that you would bring a friend to speak truth to me. Help me also to be an encouraging friend who brings peace to those around me.*

# New Every Morning

*The Lord's love never ends.*
*His mercies never stop.*
*They are new every morning.*
*Lord, your loyalty is great.*
LAMENTATIONS 3:22-23 ICB

What is the first thing you think of when you wake up in the morning? Do you think about who else is awake? Do you think about finding where your mom and dad are? Do you start to think about what you are going to have for breakfast?

Did you know that God lets you start again every day? If you had a bad day yesterday, or you did something wrong, God says that he is there to forgive you and you don't have to worry about it by the time you wake up. Try to remember that when you wake up each day, God has given you a new start!

***Father, thank you for a new day and a new start. I love you!***

# Good and Perfect

*Whatever is good and perfect is a gift coming down to us from God our Father, who created all the lights in the heavens. He never changes or casts a shifting shadow.*
JAMES 1:17 NLT

Take the next few minutes to think about all the good and beautiful things in your life. This might be easy, but maybe it is not. You might have had a bad day and don't see anything good and perfect right now. Think again!

Pretty flowers, the shape of the moon, loving and being loved, these are gifts from God. Your Father is a good father and he gives good gifts. He promises to always be good to you.

***Lord, every day you send gifts, reminding me you are good and I am yours. Thank you for loving me.***

# Truly Awesome

*The heavens tell the glory of God.*
*And the skies announce what his hands have made.*
*Day after day they tell the story.*
*Night after night they tell it again.*
PSALM 19:1-2 ICB

Amazing beauty is all around us, so much that we can become used to it. When was the last time you stopped to see just how creative God really is?

Study a flower. Read about the human eye. Watch the sun rise or set. Write down your dreams. Spend some time just being amazed at the awesomeness of the Creator.

*God, you are truly awesome. Every time I look at the sky, I see something new. How beautiful you have made this world. I am blessed to live in it.*

# No Darkness

*This is the message we have heard from him
and declare to you: God is light;
in him there is no darkness at all.*

1 JOHN 1:5 NIV

In total darkness, we look for light. We look for a light switch, open the curtains, or try to find a flashlight. As soon as a light goes on, we can see. We can find our way.

This same thing happens in our hearts. God is pure light, and with him, we can overcome any darkness we face. No wrong thing, bad words, bad actions, or fear can get in the way of his light and love.

**Father, you are all good, all pure, all light. Thank you for helping me when things feel dark, and for showing me your love.**

# Fight Evil with Good

*Submit yourselves, then, to God.*
*Resist the devil, and he will flee from you.*
JAMES 4:7 NIV

In movies, the bad guys don't give up without a fight. They try to fight good until they can't fight anymore. Thankfully, the good guys always seem a bit smarter and a bit stronger. The good guys win in the end, but they have to fight to win.

You might have realized that doing the right thing can be like getting into a fight with evil. It's really hard when you want to be angry, to shout, to have a tantrum. You have to fight those feelings and let God's goodness win! The Bible promises that when you choose good, evil will run far from you!

**Lord, give me strength to do the right thing and help me send the enemy running.**

# A Long Time Ago

*From long ago no one has ever heard*
*of a God like you.*
*No one has ever seen a God besides you.*
*You help the people who trust you.*
ISAIAH 64:4 NIV

God has been around for a really long time. Think back hundreds of years, think back thousands of years. What was life like back then? We don't know exactly, but we do know that God was around for those people too.

Ever since the beginning of creation, God has been the one true God. Some people have tried to say that he isn't, but he has shown himself to be true over thousands of years. You can trust that our God is the one true God.

**Lord, thank you that you have shown yourself to so many people since a long time ago, and that we still believe that you are the one true God today.**

# Sing Praise

*Sing praises to God. Sing praises.*
*Sing praises to our King. Sing praises.*
*God is King of all the earth.*
*So sing a song of praise to him.*

PSALM 47:6-7 ICB

You might not have the voice of an angel, but you can sing, no matter how good or bad it sounds. God created you with a voice and with lips that can praise him for all the good things he has done. God will have so much joy by your song of praise to him - it is the most beautiful thing that he can hear!

Sing praises to God. Sing, because he is good. Sing, because you understand his grace. Sing, because he is worthy!

**God, you are the king of all the earth. You have been good to me. Help me to sing and speak of your goodness!**

# NOVEMBER

Everything that God made is good.
Nothing that God made should be refused
if it is accepted with thanks to God.

1 TIMOTHY 4:4 ICB

# Dig Deep

*Let your roots grow down into him,
and let your lives be built on him. Then your faith
will grow strong in the truth you were taught,
and you will overflow with thankfulness.*

COLOSSIANS 2:7 NLT

A good climbing tree doesn't just pop up overnight. It takes years for any good tree to grow strong enough for someone to hang from its branches. Even the biggest trees don't stand a chance against strong winds if it is not planted deep into good soil.

God is the rich soil that we need to plant our roots deep down into. He will give us wisdom as long as we spend our time digging deeper into his Word.

*Lord, help me to find your goodness and love in your Word. Let me live everyday knowing and speaking your truth so I can be strong for you.*

# Every Day

> *Just as you received Christ Jesus as Lord,*
> *continue to live your lives in him.*
> COLOSSIANS 2:6 NIV

Do you remember your first day at school? You were probably nervous and excited, unsure of what was ahead. Your first day was important, but you wouldn't have learned anything from school if you just went one day and never went again.

It's the same with our relationship with Jesus. The day that you accepted Jesus into your life was such an important decision. But what is more important than your decision is that you keep loving Jesus every day of your life.

***Lord Jesus, I am so thankful that I belong to you. Help me to remember to keep you in my mind and my heart each day.***

# Satisfied

*Your love is better than life.*
*I will praise you.*
*I will praise you as long as I live.*
*I will lift up my hands in prayer to your name.*
*I will be content as if I had eaten the best foods.*
*My lips will sing. My mouth will praise you.*
PSALM 63:3-5 ICB

What could be better than spending a day at a fun park, eating all the candy you could find, and laughing with your friends?

The writer of this Bible verse thought that Jesus' love was better than anything they had ever experienced in life. Do you think you could agree with that? God is so good to you, and has amazing things planned for your life. Take some time today to thank him for the wonderful life he has for you.

**Lord, your love is better than what things in this life can give me. Let me remember that every day.**

# Chased by Grace

*Surely your goodness and love will be with me
all my life.
And I will live in the house of the Lord forever.*

PSALM 23:6 ICB

We leave footprints as we walk in the sand or mud. Have you ever trailed mud into the house and made your parents upset with you because of the mess?

God wants you to walk in the right direction. He doesn't want you to walk where there is sin. That would be like walking in dirt. The more you know about God, the more you will understand how to be loving and good like he is. The only footprints you will leave then are the ones that follow Jesus, right into his house!

***Heavenly Father, help me to follow
you as you walk beside me with
goodness and grace. Lead me to
dwell in your house forever.***

324

# Growing Seeds

*God supplies seed for the person who plants. He supplies bread for food. God will also supply and increase the amount of your seed. He will increase the results of your good works.*

2 CORINTHIANS 9:10 NIRV

A farmer sows a seed and the seed goes into the ground and grows a plant. We use the plant to feed people. It is just a tiny seed that gets planted, but a tiny seed will turn into something big!

The Bible sometimes compares our life to a seed. The things in our life that we do for God is like planting a seed. If you help a smaller child with their reading, or give a little bit of money to someone in need, there will be something bigger that comes from your small act of love. So, give in love, and watch God make it grow.

*Father, thank you for giving me love so that I can use your love to do small but wonderful things for you.*

# So Happy

*"The Lord your God is with you.*
*The mighty One will save you.*
*The Lord will be happy with you.*
*You will rest in his love.*
*He will sing and be joyful about you."*

ZEPHANIAH 3:17 ICB

Parents are very proud of their children. It doesn't matter what gift you have, your parents will always be proud of many things that you do because they completely love who you are. They see a beautiful heart and amazing potential.

Our heavenly Father feels like this about you—only much more. He is always near to you, he protects you, he is proud, and he is loving. Can you imagine him today, being so happy to be near you that he sings and rejoices over you!

*Father, sometimes I forget that you love me*
*for who I am, not what I do. You see my*
*heart and you rejoice over me!*

# Too Good for Words

*Lord our God, you have done many miracles.*
*Your plans for us are many.*
*If I tried to tell them all,*
*there would be too many to count.*

PSALM 40:5 ICB

How long do you think it would take to talk about every good thing God has done in your life? What if you added all the good things God has done in your whole family's lives? Now, what if you had to tell of every good thing that God has done for the entire world, from the moment it began?

The Bible says it would be too many things to speak about. God is just that good!

**Lord God, you are too great for words and I simply want to say that you are awesome.**

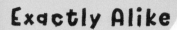

# Exactly Alike

*The Son is the shining brightness of God's glory. He is the exact likeness of God's being. He uses his powerful word to hold all things together. He provided the way for people to be made pure from sin. Then he sat down at the right hand of the King, the Majesty in heaven.*

HEBREWS 1:3 NIRV

Jesus was a special man. Did you know that the Bible says that Jesus was with God in heaven before he came to earth? Jesus was sent as a human so that everyone could experience what God was like. The Bible says that Jesus showed us God.

When you read about what Jesus did and said, remember that he was showing us what God was like. So, when Jesus told the children to come to him so he could bless them, he was showing us how much God cares for children.

**Jesus, thank you for coming to earth and showing us who God really is.**

# Continual Praise

*The Lord's name should be praised
from where the sun rises to where it sets.*
PSALM 113:3 ICB

Do you get up early enough to see the sun rise?
Are you still awake when the sun goes down? You are
probably awake the whole day, right?

The Bible says to praise God from the rising sun to
the sun that is going down. This just means that we
need to find reasons in our whole day to think about
how wonderful God is. It shouldn't be too hard. Look
at a flower or strong tree. Think about how your friend
made you laugh. Enjoy your lunch. There are so many
reasons to thank God.

***Lord, I praise you for your love for me. I pray that
you would help me to be someone that thanks
you every day.***

# The Good Father

> *"I will be your father,*
> *and you will be my sons and daughters,*
> *says the Lord All-Powerful."*
>
> 2 CORINTHIANS 6:18 ICB

God has been around for such a long time that we might think he is just an old man, like a nice old Grandpa. God is nice, but we need to remember that he is not an ordinary person. He is the king of the universe and the father of all of his creation.

God is more like a good father. He is strong, protective, and loves you no matter what. He is the heavenly Father, and this means that he is in control of everything. Will you trust him to take care of you today?

***Thank you, God, that you are a good father, and that you love me as your child.***

# Loving Right

*The Lord wants to show his mercy to you.*
*He wants to rise and comfort you.*
*The Lord is a fair God.*
*And everyone who waits for his help will be happy.*

ISAIAH 30:18 ICB

We all get grumpy sometimes. We shout, we push, we say unkind things. Usually when this happens we get in trouble. This is because adults want you to grow up into a person that treats people with kindness.

God doesn't want us to be mean either, but his first response to your grumpiness is not anger. He wants to show you love even when you have done wrong. When you feel his love, it helps you to be more kind and fair to others.

**Jesus, thank you that you show me love and not anger. Help me to be a more kind and fair person because of your love.**

# Understand Jesus

*What we have received is not the spirit of the world. We have received the Spirit who is from God. The Spirit helps us understand what God has freely given us.*

1 CORINTHIANS 2:12 NIRV

We didn't live in the days that Jesus came to earth. We know about him because there were people with him who wrote down the things that he did and said. That's why the Bible is so important; it tells us a lot about Jesus.

When Jesus left to go back to heaven, he sent his Spirit. This is a Spirit that speaks to all of us, today, so we can know all about Jesus and his way. Read the Bible today and ask the Spirit of God to speak to you so you will learn more about Jesus.

**Heavenly Father, thank you that through your spirit I can understand and accept all your good gifts.**

# Goodness in Waiting

*The Lord is wonderfully good to those who wait for him, to those who seek for him. It is good both to hope and wait quietly for the salvation of the Lord.*
LAMENTATIONS 3:25-26 TLB

Have you ever been last to be picked for a team or last to get food at the dinner table? It can be hard to be patient when you watch everyone else get what you want.

Finding yourself waiting is hard enough without watching everyone else rush ahead of you. But God promises goodness to those who are kept waiting. If you choose to think about good things as you wait, God will show you wonderful things.

*Help me, God, to see waiting as a good chance to know your goodness. Teach me to wait quietly and with hope for you.*

# Seeing Light

*You are the giver of life.*
*Your light lets us enjoy life.*

PSALM 36:9 ICB

How would you explain color to a blind person? What is blue, and what makes it different from red, purple, or green? In order to understand pink, you need to have seen it.

It is the same with goodness, love, and light. In order to understand it, we need to have seen it. In order to know it, we must know the Father. He is the one true source of all light, of all that is good.

***God, I want to live in the light! Help me to understand you by seeing your love and light all around me.***

# Best Day Ever

*A single day in your courts*
*is better than a thousand anywhere else!*
*I would rather be a gatekeeper in the house of my God*
*than live the good life in the homes of the wicked.*
PSALM 84:10 NLT

Do you remember the most awesome day you have ever had? Maybe it was a time during school vacation, or when you got a goal during your sports game. It might have been your birthday.

The Bible says that just one day in God's house is like your best day ever. You would rather have that one day than have a thousand boring days. God is so awesome that the more you get to know him, the more you want to be with him.

*Lord, I want to spend time with you. Help me to know you so well that one day with you will be my best day ever.*

# As I Should Be

*There is surely a future hope for you,*
*and your hope will not be cut off.*

**PROVERBS 23:18** NIV

God made you. Carefully and beautifully, he made you. And he knew exactly what he was doing and why. Even the desires of your heart are there for a reason: God gave you things that you would love to do and that you would be good at.

The next time you wonder if you are good enough, remember these words. Look at the things you love doing, the things you are good at doing. God has a wonderful future for you and these good things are part of his plan for you.

*Lord, thank you for reminding me that*
*I am made exactly as I should be.*
*Lead me to the good you want*
*me to do.*

# Buried Talents

*"Whoever has will be given more, and they will have an abundance. Whoever does not have, even what they have will be taken from them."*
MATHEW 25:29 NIV

What would you do if you were given a whole trunk full of precious treasure? Would you use the gold coins to buy things for you and for others? Would you wear the jewels or put the crown on? Or would you bury it in the ground so that nobody could ever see it again?

God gave you a treasure. It's called your talents—the things that you are good at. God wants you to use these talents. If you don't, it's just as silly as burying a great treasure in the ground. Nobody can use things that are buried. So keep doing those things that you are great at!

*Jesus, thanks so much for the treasure you have given me—the gifts you have created me with. Help me to use my gifts.*

# Slow Beauty

*God has shown me amazing and wonderful things. People should not think more of me because of it. So I wouldn't become proud of myself, I was given a problem. This problem caused pain in my body.*

2 CORINTHIANS 12:7 NIRV

Do you know the story of the ugly duckling? When he was little, he didn't think he looked very good like all the other beautiful swans in his pond. Then one day, after many years, he looked at his reflection in the water and realized that he had grown into a beautiful swan too!

Sometimes it is better when we don't get proud. If we were all exactly like we wanted to be we might start bragging and not be very nice people. God is going to make you beautiful and strong, but it will come from the inside out.

*Thank you, God, for not giving me everything that I want all at once. Thank you for keeping kindness in my heart.*

# Listen

*"The seed on good soil stands for those with an honest and good heart. Those people hear the message. They keep it in their hearts. They remain faithful and produce a good crop."*

LUKE 8:15 NIRV

When you plant a seed, you push it deeply into the soil. A seed won't grow if it is put on a rock because there is nothing for it to dig its roots into.

Sometimes we hear things from God, but we don't really listen. This is like being a seed that gets put on a rock. What we hear can be forgotten and we don't let our life change. When we hear God's words, we need to remember them. Write them down, memorize them. That way, you will be able to understand more about God.

*Lord, thank you that you speak to me. Thank you for your words in the Bible. Help me to remember your words so I can understand more about you.*

# A Million Plus One

*Praise the Lord!*
*Thank the Lord because he is good.*
*His love continues forever.*

PSALM 106:1 ICB

Have you ever said, "I forgive you," so many times that you get sick of it? Maybe your brother or sister has annoyed you and then said sorry. You will forgive them, but if they keep doing it, you don't want to forgive them anymore. It's frustrating!

Thankfully, our God doesn't feel like we do about forgiveness. His love for you is so great that he will forgive you every single time that you ask for forgiveness. Even if it is millions of times!

**Lord, I am so grateful that you forgive me every time I ask you to. Thank you for your mercy.**

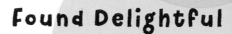

# Found Delightful

*May my friends sing and shout for joy.*
*May they always say,*
*"Praise the greatness of the Lord.*
*He loves to see his servants do well."*
PSALM 35:27 ICB

Do you shout very much? We are not usually allowed to shout when we are in a classroom or a library, and probably not at home either!

There is a reason and a time to shout though. God wants us to shout for joy when we think about how awesome he is to us. We can do this at church while we are singing, or outside, while we are enjoying God's beauty. There are plenty of places that are okay to shout—so shout for joy, today!

**God, thanks so much for the beautiful things in my life. You make me happy!**

# Stronghold

*The Lord is good.*
*He gives protection in times of trouble.*
*He knows who trusts in him.*

NAHUM 1:7 ICB

God isn't only with us in the good times. Even in the day of trouble, God knows those who trust him, and he is a safe place for them.

Not only when everything goes wrong, but even in our moments of doing wrong things, God wants to be our strength and help us figure out how to make things right. We can trust him and know that he is always good.

**Thank you, Lord, that you are a source of strength for me even when I am weak.**

# Love in Creation

*"You are worthy, our Lord and God!*
*You are worthy to receive glory and honor and power.*
*You are worthy because you created all things.*
*They were created and they exist.*
*This is the way you planned it."*

REVELATION 4:11 NIRV

Have you ever thought about just how many things God created? Think of all the animals that you can, and then think about all the sea creatures. Now think of all the different kinds of flowers, trees, countries, stars and planets.

Wow! God created so much! The best thing is he also created you, and he created others. And because God is love, he put love in the middle of all of his creation. This is what we praise him for!

**God help me to praise you for everything that you have created, including me and the other people in my life!**

# Father Knows Best

*We are confident that he hears whenever we ask for anything that pleases him. And since we know he hears us when we make our requests, we also know that he will give us what we ask for.*

1 JOHN 5:14-15 NLT

When we pray, we are heard by a God who cares a lot about what we say to him. When you know that God wants to listen to you, then you can be brave enough to ask him for things.

God is a good Father and if we ask him for things that he knows will be good for us, he will say yes! Go ahead and ask him for what you want or need, and trust that he will give you the best answer.

**Thank you, God, that you answer my prayers. Help me to trust that you know exactly what is best for me.**

# Stored Goodness

*You have stored up so many good things.*
*You have stored them up*
*for those who have respect for you.*
*You give those things while everyone watches.*
*You give them to people who run to you for safety.*
PSALM 31:19 NIRV

God is storing up goodness! What exactly is that goodness? Is it safety? Is it peace? Is it a quiet heart when life is crazy? Is it joy even when your best friend is mad at you? Yes, it would seem that his goodness could be all of these and much more.

There is so much goodness that God actually has to store it, so he doesn't overwhelm us in it all at once. The goodness is for those who know God. God will reward you more than your wildest dreams for loving him like that.

**Help me, Jesus, to trust in your goodness.**
**Thank you that you are storing up a lot**
**of good for your people.**

# Water of Life

*"Anyone who drinks the water I give them will never be thirsty. In fact, the water I give them will become a spring of water in them. It will flow up into eternal life."*

JOHN 4:14 NIRV

Wouldn't it be amazing never to have to feel hungry or thirsty? We wouldn't have to wait half an hour before swimming or get a headache because we forgot to drink water.

When we think about wanting or needing things like safety, love and comfort, Jesus said that he will never run out of giving those to us. He says that will always be there for us, like a big bottle of water that never runs out.

***Jesus, thank you that the important things in life never run out. You give me more than enough of the things I really need.***

# Hard Love

*We know what love is because Jesus Christ
gave his life for us. So we should give our lives
for our brothers and sisters.*
1 JOHN 3:16 NIRV

It was a hard experience for Jesus to have to die on the cross. It hurt him and made him feel rejected by everyone. He went through this pain because he loves us and he knew that giving us eternal life was going to be the best thing for us.

It would be pretty hard to do what Jesus did, but thankfully he only had to do that once. We don't have to die on a cross, but we do have to love people so much, just like Jesus does.

**Thank you, Jesus, for going through such a hard thing, all because you love me. Help me to love others in the same way.**

# 100 Percent

*Trust the Lord with all your heart.*
*Don't depend on your own understanding.*
*Remember the Lord in everything you do.*
*And he will give you success.*

PROVERBS 3:5-6 ICB

How do you know that the world is round? How do you know that there are planets in the sky? We have to trust that the scientists who say these things are telling the truth and know a lot of facts about the universe we live in.

We have to trust God in the same way. God is even greater than the smartest scientist in the world. He knows everything. When God says something is true, or gives his people a promise, you can believe him 100 percent!

**Heavenly Father, thank you that you know absolutely everything. Help me to trust in your ways.**

# Leading the Blind

*Then I will lead the blind along
a way they never knew.
I will guide them along paths they have not known.
I will make the darkness become light for them.
And I will make the rough ground smooth.
These are the things I will do.
I will not leave my people.*

ISAIAH 42:16 ICB

A guide dog is one of the cutest dogs, isn't it? Usually it's a black or golden little puppy with a red jacket on its back. These dogs are allowed into stores, schools, and even onto planes because they are learning how to guide blind people and make sure they don't get into danger.

God leads us like this. He makes sure that we don't get into trouble, and that we know which way to go. He can see things that we cannot see.

**Thank you, God, for your
promise to guide me.**

# It's True!

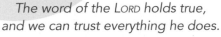

> *The word of the L*ORD* holds true,*
> *and we can trust everything he does.*
>
> PSALM 33:4 NLT

Have you ever been telling a story and other people tell you that they don't think that what you are saying is true? It can be frustrating to try to convince people that you are telling the truth. If they weren't there, or don't know much about your story, it can be a hard argument to win.

God might feel like that sometimes. We might not always believe in his promises. He wants us to know more about him so we can know for sure that his words are the truest words we will ever hear.

***God, I'm sorry when I haven't believed your promises. Help me to trust your words always.***

# DECEMBER

They speak about your glorious majesty.
I will spend time thinking about your
wonderful deeds.
They speak about the powerful and
wonderful things you do.
I will talk about the great things
you have done.
They celebrate your great goodness.
They sing for joy about your holy acts.

PSALM 145:5-7 NIRV

351

# Just Because

*Honor the LORD for the glory of his name.*
*Worship the LORD in the splendor of his holiness.*
PSALM 29:2 NLT

Isn't it cool when it isn't your birthday but someone gives you a gift anyway? It might be a normal day, but if your parents bring you home a present, it feels awesome. Surprise gifts can be the best kind of gifts.

When is the last time you surprised God by just saying that you love him? He loves to get special gifts too. Your gift to God is a simple thank you, or an "I love you just because."

*God, today I want to say that I love you. I know that you are a wonderful God and I want you to feel loved by me.*

# The Gift

*When people work, their wages are not a gift, but something they have earned. But people are counted as righteous, not because of their work, but because of their faith in God who forgives sinners.*

ROMANS 4:4-5 NLT

Have you thought about what job you might want to do when you grow up? Is it a builder, or a nurse? Do you want to work in a bank, or with animals? When you work hard in this world, you get paid for it.

Jesus says that his gift is like money that you didn't have to work for! He gave you forgiveness and eternal life, and you didn't have to do anything to get it. When you believe in Jesus, you have the greatest gift ever.

**Lord Jesus, thank you so much for giving me a gift that I didn't even work for. Help me to keep believing in you.**

# Tell Your Story

*That is what the people the Lord has saved should say.*
*They are the ones he has saved from the enemy.*
PSALM 107:2 NIV

What's your story? Where were you born? How many people are there in your family? Why do you believe in Jesus?

From the beginning, God had you in mind. He planned you out to the tiniest detail. He has loved you *forever.* Your story about your life and about how you came to love Jesus really matters, so be brave and share it!

**Lord, sometimes I think my story isn't really important, but remind me that I have a wonderful story to tell. Help me to be brave and share my story about you with others.**

# I Am Found

*"Rejoice with me; I have found my lost sheep."*
LUKE 15:6 NIV

It feels so good to find something that you thought you had lost! We feel happy when we find something even if it is small, like your favorite pencil, book, or pair of sunglasses. It could be something bigger too, like a pet.

A farmer feels like that when he has lost an animal. In the Bible, Jesus talked about a shepherd who had lost his sheep and went looking for it. Everyone cares about things that belong to them. That's why Jesus says that he celebrates when he goes looking for people that love him and finds them, even if it is just one!

**Jesus, thank you that came looking for me. I belong to you and you care about me.**

# Jesus Helps

*The Lord gives sight to the blind.*
*The Lord lifts up people who are in trouble.*
*The Lord loves those who do right.*
PSALM 146:8 ICB

There were a lot of people that needed help when Jesus was on earth. People needed to be healed from sickness and poor people needed help to live. Jesus didn't forget about the people that were doing the right thing either. He knew that life could be hard for those who were following him.

Are there ways that you can be like Jesus? Can you find someone who is sick to pray for? Can you give something to someone who doesn't have much? There are a lot of people that need help in our world today, and we have something very special to give them—the love of Jesus.

*Jesus, thank you for caring for everybody. Help me to see the needs in my world and to help where I can.*

# Love Others

*Pay everything you owe. But you can never pay back all the love you owe one another. Whoever loves other people has done everything the law requires.*

ROMANS 13:8 NIRV

Jesus doesn't have many rules for us. He doesn't make us pay him back or work extra hard for doing wrong things. There is one thing that he thinks we need to do. We need to love others.

It might seem like an easy rule, but when you think about loving people that have hurt you, or people that you don't like, that's when the rule gets hard. Jesus loves us no matter what, and we need to learn to show love to others in whatever way we can.

**Jesus, you amaze me with the love that you have for me. Help me to love others all the time.**

# He Will Be Back

*The Lord is not slow to keep his promise. He is not slow in the way some people understand it. Instead, he is patient with you. He doesn't want anyone to be destroyed. Instead, he wants all people to turn away from their sins.*

2 PETER 3:9 NIRV

When your parents go out for dinner, they might leave you with a babysitter or maybe your grandparents. They are out for a little while, but they always come back.

Jesus will come back to earth one day. He promised he would! It might seem like a long time while we are waiting for him to come back, but we still need to believe that he will because he always keeps his promises.

*Jesus, thank you that you will come back one day. Help me to be someone that shares your hope with others.*

# Nothing Can Stop It

*I am absolutely sure that not even death or life can separate us from God's love. Not even angels or demons, the present or the future, or any powers can separate us. Not even the highest places or the lowest, or anything else in all creation can separate us. Nothing at all can ever separate us from God's love. That's because of what Christ Jesus our Lord has done.*

ROMANS 8:38-39 NIRV

Our friendship with Jesus Christ is forever. You may have just started to know Jesus, or you might have been his friend since you were a baby. It doesn't matter how long you have known him, he is going to love you forever!

Jesus isn't exactly like the friends you have now. He doesn't get mad at you. He doesn't choose other friends and exclude you. He doesn't boss you around. He just loves you, and nothing is going to stop his love!

***Jesus, thank you that you will love me forever!***

# Returned Love

*I love those who love me,
and those who seek me find me.*
PROVERBS 8:17 NIV

When you have been in a fight and go off to a different place, like your room or the other side of the playground, your friend or brother or sister might try to come and find you to make things right. When people come to find you, you feel really cared for.

Jesus wants to be found. He is never hiding, but he wants you to come to him and make things right. He is always ready to forgive you and he will tell you that he has never stopped loving you.

*Jesus, help me to always look for where you are. I know that you are near, but I know that you want me to come and spend time with you. I love you.*

# His Riches

*This same God who takes care of me will supply all your needs from his glorious riches, which have been given to us in Christ Jesus.*

PHILIPPIANS 4:19 NLT

God is always able to give you what you need. Sometimes we may feel like we don't deserve things from God. Sometimes we find it hard to trust, and we worry about our needs.

The good news is that Jesus said you can come to him and ask for what you need at any time. You are a child of the king and he offers his riches to you. All you need to do is love him, ask him, and trust in his goodness. He promises to take care of you.

**God, you are so good. Thank you that you want to take care of me.**

# Show Love

*"All people will know that you are my followers
if you love each other."*

JOHN 13:35 NCV

What makes you realize that you are loved? Is it a hug, or a smile meant just for you? Sometimes we get nice notes, or kind words. Maybe you can remember a time when you fell over and somebody helped you up, or took you to an adult who could take care of you.

There are hundreds of ways to show love. God said that if we show love to one another, people will notice. It's a great thing if people notice your kindness because that is how people start to believe that God is good.

*God, I want to be known as your follower. Teach me to love like you so I can show your love to those around me.*

# Fighting By Your Side

*The LORD is faithful; he will strengthen you
and guard you from the evil one.*
2 THESSALONIANS 3:3 NLT

Faithful friends always stands up for you. A faithful dog sticks close to your side. God is faithful. He will never leave your side. Even if you feel like you are in the middle of a battle, he will be right there, fighting with you.

If you feel like people are saying mean things about you, God will remind you of what he loves about you. If you feel like nobody cares, God will remind you that he does. He will always help you find joy and peace in your life.

**God, I feel stronger knowing that you are right by my side. Please give me peace and joy when I am feeling down.**

# Full of Love

*Satisfy us in the morning with your unfailing love,*
*that we may sing for joy and be glad all our days.*
Psalm 90:14 NIV

You know when you have eaten so much that you feel too full to eat anymore? It might have been a really yummy dinner and you ate so much that you felt like you were going to burst. But then the ice-cream comes out and you think maybe you do have enough space to eat a bit more.

God's love can fill us up to the brim, and just when we think we have had enough, he gives us even more. Let yourself be full of his love so that you are always ready to share it.

**Lord, my heart is full of your love, but I always want more. Help me to share this love with my friends, family, and others in my life.**

# Great Love

*He loves those who have respect for him.*
*His love is as high as the heavens are above the earth.*
PSALM 103:11 NIRV

Did you know it would take the fastest spaceship almost ten years to travel to Pluto (that's the furthest known planet away from the Sun)? That's pretty far away, and that's just a planet. There is so much more to God's universe, and this is how big the Bible says his love is for us!

He is a great and wonderful God. He is great in how much he has created, but also great in how much he loves you.

***Father God, you are amazing! When I think about everything you have made, I am so grateful that you chose to love me.***

# My King

*Your eyes will see the king in his beauty.*
*You will see the land that stretches far away.*
ISAIAH 33:17 ICB

We don't get to see kings much these days, but you have probably heard lots of stories about them. Kings owned all of the land that surrounded them and they had all of the power over the people. They lived in big castles and had all the riches they could ever want.

People of the Bible really wanted to have a king. They wanted someone who would rule over them in a fair and kind way. They wanted someone who would protect them from their enemies and bring them joy and peace. These people finally got their wish. God sent Jesus to be the king over everyone. He is the king that, one day, you will finally see.

***Thank you, that I will see your face one day and walk with you in your kingdom.***

# Talk to Jesus

*Because of Christ and our faith in him, we can now come boldly and confidently into God's presence.*
EPHESIANS 3:12 NLT

Do you think a baby or a toddler knows the difference between a normal man and a king? Probably not! A toddler would talk the same way to both people. Wouldn't it be funny to see a little baby poke his tongue out at a king or queen?

Jesus said that we can come to him like little children. That means that we don't need to be afraid of him, or worry about what he will think of us. We can just be ourselves. Be brave, and go talk to Jesus about anything!

**Jesus, I come to you now and ask you to take care of me. I am so glad that you hear me and answer me.**

# Found in a Desert

*He found them in a desert,*
*a windy, empty land.*
*He surrounded them and brought them up,*
*guarding them as those he loved very much.*
DEUTERONOMY 32:10 NCV

In the Bible, God's people, the Israelites, spent a lot of time wandering around in the desert, waiting to be led into the promised land. The desert would not be a very nice place to live. It is hot and dry with no food or water. Even though it was kind of their fault for being there, God went and found the Israelites and took care of them. Finally, they were able to get to the promised land.

Sometimes you have to wait for God. You might feel like you are lost and alone, but God will find you and he will bring you out of a bad place into something much better.

**Thank you, Father, that you will find me if I ever lose my way. Help me to trust that you love me.**

# Collected Tears

*You have seen me tossing and turning through the night. You have collected all my tears and preserved them in your bottle! You have recorded every one in your book.*

PSALM 56:8 TLB

Don't be afraid to come to God with your cares. Share with him the deepest feelings in your heart without holding back. In his presence you will find comfort, hope, compassion, and more love than you could imagine.

God longs to comfort us: to stroke our hair, wipe our tears, and hold us in his arms. He counts the nights we have bad dreams; he collects our tears. God isn't far away when we are sad—he is closer than ever.

**Thank you, Jesus, for holding me in my sadness. I need your strength even more in those times. Please be near to me and comfort me.**

# The Gift of Peace

*"Give glory to God in heaven,
and on earth let there be peace among
the people who please God."*

LUKE 2:14 NCV

Christmas trees might not be from the Bible, but they bring Christians thoughts of a more precious tree: the cross. Jesus came to us to bring peace to his people through the cross.

Jesus was on a mission to rescue us from every thought, word, or action that didn't match up with God's goodness. He took all of those evil things with him on the cross and got rid of them for good. Jesus made a way for goodness to come back into the human heart. Our hearts, full of peace, is a Christmas gift for each of us to open every day.

*Father, thank you for the gift of peace I can have when I choose to believe in you.*

# The Gift of Joy

*I loved you as the Father loved me. Now remain in my love I have obeyed my Father's commands, and I remain in his love. In the same way, if you obey my commands, you will remain in my love. I have told you these things so that you can have the same joy I have. I want your joy to be the fullest joy.*

JOHN 15:9-11 ICB

Joy comes into our lives when we follow God's directions. God rewards us with a whole lot of love. As we stay in this love, we become full of joy that can be shared with the people around us.

Can you think of anyone that needs more joy in their life? The days leading up to Christmas can be fun, but they can also be stressful for adults. Maybe you could help them by being a happy person to be around.

**Thank you, Lord, for your love that gives me joy. Help me to share my joy with those around me.**

# The Gift of Charity

*Suppose a believer is rich enough to have all that he needs. He sees his brother in Christ who is poor and does not have what he needs. What if the believer does not help the poor brother? Then the believer does not have God's love in his heart. My children, our love should not be only words and talk. Our love must be true love. And we should show that love by what we do.*

1 John 3:17-18 icb

The Christmas season is filled with chances to give. Have you seen people outside stores with buckets to collect money? Many stores let you buy presents for children who wouldn't usually get them because their families don't have much.

Christmas is a time to be very thankful for what you have, and then to think about what other people might need. Remember to share your love, your time, and your gifts with others.

**God, show me the people around me who need extra help. Let me show charity to them in some way.**

374

# The Gift of Faithfulness

*"I have brought you glory on earth
by finishing the work you gave me to do."*
JOHN 17:4 NIV

You know when you have been asked to do a task, like your homework, or clearing away the dishes? It feels good to finish something that you knew you were supposed to do. Faithfulness is all about sticking to what you said you were going to do.

Jesus had to be faithful as well. Going to the cross was not an easy thing for him to finish, but he knew that it was God's plan. So, he finished the task that God gave him. Because of his faithfulness, we now have eternal life with him.

*Jesus, thank you so much for finishing the work you had to do on the cross. Your faithfulness is a gift to me.*

# Good News!

*The shepherds went quickly and found Mary and Joseph. And the shepherds saw the baby lying in a feeding box. Then they told what the angels had said about this child. Everyone was amazed when they heard what the shepherds said to them.*

LUKE 2:16-18 ICB

When the shepherds were told about Jesus, they ran to him! They ran as fast as their feet could carry them. They rushed to Bethlehem and into his barn stall to see him. After they had seen the baby, they knew he was the savior of the world and they went to tell everyone about him!

Doesn't it seem surprising that God chose ordinary people to spread his message? We should be grateful that he does! Hallelujah! Christ has come! Tell your friends. Tell your neighbors. Tell everyone you meet— Jesus is the Lord, and he has come to give us life!

**Lord Jesus, thank you for coming to give the whole world new life. I will tell about your goodness as long as I live.**

# Every Detail

*The LORD makes secure the footsteps*
*of the person who delights in him,*
*Even if that person trips, he won't fall.*
*The LORD's hand takes good care of him.*
PSALM 37:23-24 NIRV

The day after Christmas is very exciting! You get to play with all your new things and enjoy the gifts you have been given. When you first get something new you play with it a lot and you learn about its every detail.

Jesus is excited about you all of the time. He doesn't only care about the big stuff, he cares about the details. He cares when you make a good choice, when you feel sad, and when you fall down. He says that he takes you by the hand and lifts you back up again.

**Thank you, Jesus, that you are excited about me. Help me to listen to you and know how to follow you.**

# A God Coat

*You were taught to start living a new life. It is created to be truly good and holy, just as God is.*
Ephesians 4:24 NIRV

You have to decide what to wear most days by looking at the weather outside. Is it cold, raining, hot, windy? We have clothes for almost every kind of weather. You wouldn't put on a rain coat in the middle of a hot day. You wouldn't wear a t-shirt if it were snowing!

When God gave us a new life in him, he said we can put him on, kind of like a coat. We can wake up each morning, decide that we want to be like God, and remind our hearts and minds to be true and right.

**Jesus, thank you for being true and right. Help me to wake up every morning and choose to put my God-coat on!**

# Coming Soon

*Always be full of joy in the Lord; I say it again, rejoice! Let everyone see that you are unselfish and considerate in all you do. Remember that the Lord is coming soon. Don't worry about anything; instead, pray about everything; tell God your needs, and don't forget to thank him for his answers.*

PHILIPPIANS 4:4-6 TLB

Do you like when you have friends or relatives coming over to your house? It's exciting as you prepare for them to arrive. You might clean your room or help your parents get the food ready. You might set up a game to play.

We have a promise that Jesus will come back one day. That should fill us with happiness and excitement! While you are waiting, remember there are things to do. Be kind to people. Show the love of God to others. Pray about everything. Get ready for the return of Jesus!

*God, I am so thankful that you promised to come back. Help me not to worry about how it is all going to work out, but instead to pray about everything.*

# Standing Strong

*"Man must not live only on bread. He must also live on every word that comes from the mouth of God."*
MATTHEW 4:4 NIRV

Do you know the story of when Jesus was tempted by the devil? Jesus had gone to the desert for forty days and he chose not to eat anything during that time. He must have felt quite weak! At the end of that time, Satan came to tempt him. He offered him the whole world if Jesus would just turn a rock into bread. But Jesus knew what the Satan was up to—he wanted to turn Jesus away from his mission.

Jesus used the words of God to defeat Satan. That is exactly what we can do when we are tempted to do wrong. Read your Bible and pray. Get full of God's words so that you are strong!

*Father, thank you that you have given me your words. Help me to read and listen to those words so I can stand strong against the enemy.*

# He Blesses Me

*Praise the Lord!*
*Happy is the person who fears the Lord.*
*He loves what the Lord commands.*
PSALM 112:1 ICB

Blessings from God are gifts that he gives us because he loves us. When you respect him, and choose to accept his love, you will want to obey him from your heart.

The Lord wants to bless you so that you can bless others. Walk closely with God so that you don't miss the chance to bless those close to you.

***Lord, thank you that you give me blessings because I want to please you. Help me to share these blessings with others.***

# Showing kindness

*"Is there anyone still left in Saul's family? I want to show kindness to this person for Jonathan's sake!"*
2 Samuel 9:1 icb

When you meet your friend's brother or sister, father or mother, you know that you should be polite and nice, because you want to do the right thing for your friend.

King David did this in the Bible. He loved his friend Jonathan so much that he asked if there was anyone else that he could be kind to, because he wanted Jonathan to be pleased. What would happen if you asked that question? Is there anyone you can show kindness to today?

*Lord, remind me to ask who I can show kindness to. Help me to listen to your voice and to be a great friend to others.*